Images and Echoes

Short Stories
by John Muniz

To Joyce
I'm sure I could not have done it without your guidance & support.
Many thanks
John Muniz

Images and Echoes

Copyright 1997
by
John Muniz

Library of Congress Catalog Card Number
96-62013

ISBN: 1-890306-00-2

No portion of this book
may be reproduced
without the written permission
of the author

Warwick House

Publishing

720 Court Street
Lynchburg, Virginia

Dedication

Anyone who writes is forever indebted
to those who taught us and encouraged our effort.
But we owe the most to those who love us,
who bear with our struggles and frustrations
yet never lose faith, nor allow us to.

This book is dedicated to my wife, Doris,
my sons Tom and Dave, their wives Susie and Catherine,
and all my wonderful grandchildren.

Contents

Images and Echoes 1

An Arrangement 2

Rossi's Raiders 10

Rainbow's End 19

Singular Choices 22

Talk 34

Getting Even 41

The Searchers 50

Rachel's Run 57

Something of Consequence 69

The Outsider 81

A Second Chance 87

Images and Echoes

I conjure up the images of folks that I once knew
And the echoes of the tales they had to tell
To recreate the magic of things that once we shared
As the murmurs from the mist now weave their spell

An Arrangement

$\mathcal{B}$arney Tilman could hear the phone ringing as he fumbled with the key to unlock his office door. He hurried in and grabbed the phone across the desk.

"This is Chief Tilman."

"Would you please tell me what's going on down there in your Department?"

The voice on the phone didn't wait for an answer nor bother to identify the speaker, but just continued on in the same querulous tone, "I just heard about Walter Jarvik and the incident he had with one of your people. He's really upset."

"He should be upset, George. He's facing a DUI citation."

"Oh, come on, Barney, you can't be serious. What happened?"

"Mr. Jarvik was stopped for driving erratically at about three this morning. He refused a breath test, even though he admitted to the officer that he'd been drinking. The report indicates a noticeable odor of alcohol."

"So, who was the arresting officer?"

"Officer Ramey, Michael Ramey."

"Isn't he the one they call Mr. Clean around town?"

"I don't know what they call him around town. What are you getting at, George?"

"Nothing, nothing! It's just that with Jarvik leading the opposition on council this puts me — and you too — in an awkward position."

"Really? How so?"

"Well, you know, it might look like you, ah, we might've been on the lookout for him."

"Now look here! You know I've worked for years to make this department apolitical. I think I've finally got the principle across to the rank and file. Don't you give me any of that 'we' garbage. You, and he and anyone else can think whatever they damn well please."

"Calm down, Barney."

"Calm down, hell! Jarvik calls me at home at 6:30 AM to register a complaint, and you're on the horn just as soon as I walk through the door this morning. And you tell me I should calm down." He walked gingerly around the desk, carefully lifting the phone cord over the things on his desk and sat down.

"Look Chief, Walter Jarvik has asked for a meeting this morning at eleven. He wants to go over what happened last night. He feels there might have been a ... misunderstanding of some sort."

"Is that what he told you, George?"

"Well, no. Irv Simon is the one who talked to me about the meeting."

"You mean Counselor Irving Simon is trying to arrange this meeting for Jarvik?"

"Well, yes, but..."

"Mr. Mayor, I will not attend that meeting. And if you're smart, neither will you. Jarvik is trying to have this citation tried in your office. It can only end up spelling trouble. I won't have anything to do with it."

"Now Barney, let's not jump the gun on this."

"I mean it, George. You tell Walter Jarvik I'll meet with him in my office at eleven if he wants to. But you better make it clear that if his lawyer's along I won't talk to him."

"Hey, Chief! Do you really think this approach is wise?"

"I sure as hell do, Mr. Mayor. By the way, have you discussed any of this with the town attorney? If not, I think you really ought to... even before you talk to Simon or Jarvik about anything else."

"Maybe you're right, Barney. I'll get back to you."

"You do that."

Barney Tilman replaced the phone and grabbed the sheaf of papers from his incoming basket. He began turning back sheet after sheet until he found the citation report on Walter Jarvik. He read through it quickly and then again carefully, going over each detail. He made one or two penciled notes in the margin and finally set it aside. He turned his chair to face the window. His office was in the front of the Town Hall so he could look across the street to the small park with the band shell and monuments. It was a nice little town, he thought. More like a small city, really. It sure wasn't a big city, though the politics were pretty much the same.

Hermitage always had its respectable end of town even in the years it was a sleepy farm market kind of place. The north end along the river had the reputation, even then, as being a less desirable place to live. The war had brought changes as new industry flourished along both banks of the river and began to spread toward Kelsoe, fifteen or so miles to the north. New people came to work in the plants, and the town grew too quickly, as so many towns did in those years. Kelsoe went on to become a bigger, more heavily industrialized community. And that suited the folks in Hermitage just fine. Enough remained in Hermitage to keep the town comfortably prosperous. Hermitage became a bedroom community for many of the plant workers and professional types who commuted to Kelsoe and even as far as Edgeton.

No one felt culturally deprived. Edgeton was only thirty-eight miles to the northwest. Most folks seemed just as happy to get out of town for any of their serious recreational activities. After all, Hermitage just wasn't big enough for anyone to get lost in the crowd.

The town had its country clubs, two of them in fact. And as you might have guessed, one was more exclusive than the other. Hermitage also had a string of honky-tonks scattered throughout the north end and across the river toward Kelsoe. There were ample opportunities for a variety of homegrown indiscretions. Those who frequented these places might be a little less sophisticated about their foibles, but they didn't have a corner on the market. Trouble was, too many of the southenders seemed to think if you had enough money it excused about anything.

Take the incident last night. Here we have a pillar of the community, a member of the Town Council and suave businessman, apprehended DUI, who's suddenly unhappy. He's threatened the arresting officer with his political clout, tried to intimidate the mayor, and, Barney suspected, he'll be in sometime today to put the pressure on me.

It's kind of funny, he thought, I've been here almost fifteen years as Chief of Police, and in many ways I'm still considered a "Johnny-come-lately." I'm still that "cop" from New York City who came in and took over. There was a lot of resentment back then, and things were a little dicey for the first couple of years. But I guess most of it evened out over the years. A few of the old timers still aren't members of my fan club, probably never will be either. He sighed and pulled himself back to the present. As he turned to his desk to begin his work routine the phone rang. It was the duty dispatcher.

"Mr. Jarvik for you on line one, Chief."

He punched the button and picked up the receiver, "Chief Tilman."

"Good morning again, Chief. I'd like to apologize for my early call this morning. I was a little upset. I guess I wasn't thinking too clearly."

"No problem, Mr. Jarvik. I was up."

"Good, then I didn't waken you. Perhaps you'd have some time to talk with me this morning, say about eleven? I'd really like your input on last night's incident."

Barney paused, searching for some tactful way of telling Walter Jarvik he didn't want his lawyer present, when Mr. Jarvik added, "I'd like it to be between us, Chief, off the record so to speak. Can you work it into your schedule?"

Barney was smiling as he answered, "Eleven will be fine, Mr. Jarvik. I'll see you then."

—•••••—

Walter Jarvik had that well-fed, well-groomed look of the prosperous business professional. The Chief suspected he'd probably had an hour or so in the sauna at his club before this meeting. He sat across from Barney looking fit and tan. It took a close look at the eyes to reveal the traces of his recent drinking. Barney got right to the point, "What can I do for you, Mr. Jarvik?"

"Well, it's about last night. I think there may have been a misunderstanding. I only had a couple of drinks during the course of the evening, and I had a big dinner. So I don't feel I was incapable of driving."

"You could have taken the breath test and set the whole affair to rest." He paused and asked, "Why didn't you?"

"Well, to be honest, I didn't like the officer's attitude. I felt the whole procedure was degrading."

"If you would like to file a complaint against the officer regarding his professional conduct I'll be glad to follow through on it."

"No, no! It doesn't warrant that type of action. It has more to do with the procedure for people who refuse the breath test."

"I'm sorry, but you know the law, Mr. Jarvik. How do you suggest we resolve the situation?"

"I don't know, really." He paused, "Couldn't you talk to Officer Ramey? Maybe I could apologize for my, ah... loss of temper. He might want to, ah... reconsider."

The Chief leaned forward, resting his arms on the desk. He smiled sympathetically. "Look, Mr. Jarvik, we've been around, and we both know it's a nothing-for-nothing world. If it's a compromise you're after maybe we should look at all the angles."

Jarvik nodded, smiling, and settled back in his chair. He seemed to relax and look a little more at ease. Barney Tilman continued, speaking more softly now with an air of confidentiality.

"You know, I've got thirty-eight officers on the force, as broad a spectrum of personalities as you could imagine. I've got hot-dogs and hot-shots, cynics and idealists, career cops and opportunists. I even have a couple of hard cases who like ordering people around and are only too willing to follow through with a little force. Mike Ramey happens to be one of the idealists, and he has the makings of a career officer as well. From his report, he gave you one warning only about a month ago. For him that's a pretty big concession." He smiled slightly and asked, "Just what have you got to offer, Mr. Jarvik?"

Walter Jarvik's eyes opened wide for a moment and then closed halfway. His head tilted a little to one side as he looked into the eyes of Barney Tilman. The corners of his mouth turned up ever so slightly. The Chief couldn't help thinking how much he looked like a big, contented tomcat. The silence hung between them like a presence as they sat motionless for what seemed like a long time. Finally Walter Jarvik broke the spell.

"Just what is it you want, Chief?"

"There isn't anything at all that I want."

"All right then, what does Officer Ramey want?"

"I couldn't rightly say for sure. I'm pretty sure I know what he wouldn't want, and that's for someone to offer him money to alter his citation."

Jarvik reacted angrily, "What in hell is this, some kind of game we're playing? You're talking in circles. If there's something tangible you can suggest to remedy this situation I'd like to hear it. If not, please, just say so. And I want to go on record that I had no intention at all of offering money."

Barney Tilman sat calmly and showed no reaction to the outburst. "Look, Mr. Jarvick, you were the one who requested this meeting. You've asked me some questions about one of my officers, and I've tried to respond honestly. You've asked what Mike Ramey wanted, and I told you what I thought he didn't want. Now I'll tell you what I think he does want. I think Officer Ramey wants to be seen as a good cop, one who does his job impartially for the good of the community. He wants what we all want: to be able to take care of his family in some sort of decent fashion, to be respected for his contribution to society and to feel he has somewhere to go in his chosen career."

Walter Jarvik broke in, "So, what you're telling me is, if I back the Mayor's plan for a raise in municipal salaries, something can be worked out. Right?"

"Wrong! You don't listen so well, and you interrupted me before I was finished. The point I'm trying to make is that there isn't anything you can offer Mike Ramey, or me, that will make a difference. The citation was written, and it will stand or fall in court on its own merit."

Walter Jarvik scowled and started to rise from his chair.

"Wait a minute, Mr. Jarvik. I'd like to offer a suggestion you might find helpful — and to your advantage as well."

"Some more games, Chief?"

"No, I assure you what I'm about to suggest is to be taken seriously. It may prove to be to your benefit, in the long run."

Mr. Jarvik sat back and waited. The look of anger had changed to one of annoyance, but his curiosity had been piqued. The Chief got up and walked to the window. He was turned away so neither of them had a face to read.

"It's no big secret around town that you have political aspirations beyond Hermitage, and that's fine with me. But, if my memory serves me, you did poorly in the working class areas last election. The first and second wards."

Jarvik started to reply, but the Chief held up his hand and continued, "Now if, as rumor has it, you're thinking of running for County office, you're going to have to have the working class votes not only from Hermitage, but a whole lot of votes from across the river. That includes the working stiffs from around Kelsoe and all the way up to Edgeton. Am I right?"

There was a grunt of affirmation from Jarvik.

"Frankly, Mr. Jarvik, you have the reputation for being a 'stuffed shirt' to these people. They see you as one of the 'fat-cat southenders' who think they're better than most everybody else."

"Well, that's just too damned bad what they think," Mr. Jarvick snorted.

"Yes it is, mostly because it's going to cost you votes, not only here in town, but out in the county too. It might even cost you the election." Barney rocked back and forth, hand tucked into his back pockets, still facing the window. "As I see the situation, if you plead guilty to driving while impaired — yeah, that's a reduction in charge which I might be able to arrange — you're going to look a little more human to those working stiffs. Especially if you handle it right."

Walter Jarvik suddenly looked alert and interested, "Just what do you mean by handle it right?"

"Well, suppose you go before Judge Reitman or Judge Rolfe and plead guilty. You make some kind of statement about not realizing how easy it was to fall into this trap. You commend the officer for not only upholding the law, but also for helping you realize the seriousness of the situation for yourself and for other drivers." He turned from the window and looked at the man in the chair. "Hell! I don't have to tell you how to do this, you're a past master at it. I've seen you in action on a number of occasions."

Walter Jarvik's expression changed from skepticism to reflection. He looked past the Chief out the window, weighing the feasibility of what he'd just heard. Barney waited, leaning on the back of his chair, watching the thought process unfolding.

Finally, Walter Jarvik shifted his gaze back to the chief and asked,

"This conversation stays confidential?"
The Chief nodded.
"Even from Officer Ramey... especially from him?"
Barney Tilman nodded again.
"I have your word on it?"
"You have my word on it."

—•••••—

The Clarion-Democrat carried a piece this morning about a statement made in court by Walter Jarvik who had been fined fifty dollars for operating a vehicle while impaired. Mr. Jarvik showed remorse for his actions and made a statement commending the professionalism and dedication of the arresting officer.

WHKE-TV aired a clip of Councilman Jarvik shaking Officer Ramey's hand as they stood on the steps of the Court House. The six o'clock news reported the Councilman's Court appearance, and his statement to the court.

Rossi's Raiders

Joe Rossi looked up from the clip board and tilted his head down a little to peer over his glasses at the people clustered around the table.

"We may not change anything, but we can do a couple of things, like make them notice we're here and maybe shake things up a little bit. How do you feel about it?"

There was a shuffling and shifting around in the chairs. Everyone seemed to be waiting for someone else to begin.

"I say let's go for it," George Riley was the first to answer. "What have we got to lose except the time it takes, and we all have plenty of that." There were nods of agreement.

"Well, how are we going to work it out? I mean, how will we know when we're supposed to go in there?" As usual, Mary Riley wanted particulars.

"We'll make up a schedule, so we'll know who's supposed to go on what day. No big deal!" Frank Almond, the accountant, had it all worked out in his mind.

Joe Rossi shook his head, and the comments dwindled away to silence. "Look, if we work out a schedule, say George and Mary on Mondays, another two or three on Tuesday and so on through the week, we won't accomplish anything. Sure, it'll be an inconvenience to have a couple of their machines tied up for a while, but they'll be able to work around it."

"So, what do we do?" Sam Gordon wanted to know. Small, bald and pugnacious, everything Sam did or said bordered on a challenge.

Joe was pacing back and forth in front of the table waiting for everyone to get quiet. When he felt he had their attention he grinned a little and nodded quietly.

"What we do is have the whole crowd show up on a specific day, say a Tuesday or a Wednesday. We struggle in, couples or threesomes spread out over a half hour, say 11:45 to 12:15. We tie up seven or eight of their machines, the bikes, the treadmills, the Nautilus weights, and we slowly — notice I said slowly — have a workout. You follow what I'm saying?"

"Sure, we screw up their schedule so the 'Yuppie' lunch crowd can't use the equipment." Sam was grinning, "Good plan, Joe."

"But we can't do this every day, Joe. None of us are up to it. If I use the exercise bike for half an hour I'll have sore buns for a week," Sally Simon complained.

George added, "Yeah! With my bad back the weights are a no-no. I think I can manage the bikes though."

Helen Gordon, who had been quietly taking it all in, suddenly added a new thought, "When Sam and I were in a week or so ago trying out the bikes, that trainer, you know, the one with the mustache and the muscles, hinted that we should come other than at lunch time since we had so much free time. Sam asked him if there was anything wrong with our membership. He never answered. He just left."

"That's just it," Joe added. "Since we were forced to buy full membership we can use the equipment when it suits us, not them."

Sam wanted more details. "All of us can't come everyday. How's it going to work?"

"We keep the schedule as erratic as possible: three or four individuals a couple of days a week, six or eight or as many as we can get another day, and then nobody for a couple of days. If we could get a good crowd to tie up the place, say three days in a row, we'd have them talking to themselves. You see, if we give them a pattern they can maybe plan around it, but if we hit them this way they'll never be able to do anything but react." Joe Rossi was enjoying himself.

George was laughing as he said, "Kind of like guerrilla warfare. Right?"

Sam pointed out, "The 'Yuppies' and the suits who want to maintain an exercise routine aren't going to like it. Is that the objective, Joe?"

"That's the objective," Joe nodded. "When us geriatrics were content to paddle around in the heated pool on a limited membership there were no problems. Management had to get greedy and squeeze full memberships out of us, figuring we were too old and creaky to want to use anything else. Now we need to show them what a bad decision that was. Just remember what I said about it not changing anything in the long run."

— • • • • • —

Sam and Helen strolled into the exercise room about 11:55 and scanned the equipment to see what was open. Sally Simon was already on an exercise bike peddling slowly away. She grinned and nodded toward the attendant who was watching them. Joe Rossi was walking a treadmill set on the lowest speed and holding an animated conversation with George Riley on the next machine. Marty Quinn, an ex-cop from New Jersey, was adjusting the weights on the Nautilus in preparation for his workout. Helen moved to a bike alongside Sally, and Sam started using the wall pulley weights. After two or three pulls he called to the attendant.

"Say Dennis, this is a little too much weight for me. Could you take it down, please?"

The frowning young man with the muscular build of a weight lifter sauntered over to relocate the pins in the weight pack. He was annoyed and made no effort to hide it. He bit at his mustache once or twice and mumbled to himself.

"Beg your pardon?" Sam asked.

Dennis took the bait, "I don't see why you people can't arrange to use this equipment some other time of day."

Sam stopped pulling and stood, hands on hips, "What's the matter with right now? You saying my membership is limited to specific hours?" Dennis just shook his head and walked toward the doorway where the lunch time crowd was filtering in.

Most of the equipment was now in use and there was a scramble for the few remaining stations. The others milled about in small groups, offering comments and glancing repeatedly at the big clock above the door.

At 12:18 Joe left the treadmill and waved to the others with the "I love you" gesture in sign language. One by one within the next ten minutes the others relinquished the equipment and sauntered toward the locker room.

Joe was the last one to make it back to the recreation room at the Senior Center. The others were talking quietly when he came in, and they all turned to hear what he had to say.

"Well, it's only been three days, and we've got them wondering. Monday our being there was a minor annoyance, Thursday was an inconvenience, but today was a real pain in the ass for them."

There was laughter and comments from just about everyone. Joe, grinning, waited until they calmed down. "On my way out Dennis and that muscular moron, what's-his-name, Wade, were in 'Iron Ass's' glassed-in office having a conference. Dennis was waving his hands around as he jabbered away. I waved to them as I went by, and they just glared at me."

Sally said, "I'm so sore. I don't know if I can keep this up."

"You'll have the whole weekend to recuperate. Just don't lay around, it'll only make it worse," Frank said.

"Yeah, walk it off, a little bit every day," Mary added. "How's everyone else doing?"

"Hell, we're all a little creaky and sore I guess," Marty said, "But I haven't slept so well in I can't remember when."

Joe interrupted the flurry of conversation, "I met a guy from the Spotswood Center — you know, off Raughter Road. He thinks he and his wife would like to ah... join the fun. And he thinks he can get another couple to help out. Right now there's nine of us when we're out in force. If we add four more we could tie up just about everything. Should we count them in?"

The nods, laughter and applause indicated unanimity.

"One thing," Joe cautioned, "They'll be looking for us on Monday again next week. If it's OK with everyone let's none of us show up at the club on Monday and we'll hit them on Tuesday. What's your pleasure?"

Frank Almond broke into the babble of conversation with a mock announcement, "Rossi's Raiders will strike again on Tuesday at 11:45." He flashed the "I love you" sign, and they all waved it back amidst the laughter.

Week two began on Tuesday and continued straight through Thursday. On Wednesday some of the lunch crowd began to complain to Dennis and Wade. None of the Raiders paid any attention to the turmoil, going quietly and slowly through their workouts. When they began to finish, one by one, around 12:20, those waiting began to squabble over the equipment as it became available.

On Monday of week three Wade stood in the doorway of the exercise room and told the group the room was closed for some maintenance. Sam Gordon wasn't buying it.

"When is it going to be open again?" he wanted to know.

"I don't know," Wade said. "You'll have to talk to Dennis."

Mary and Sally came out of the ladies locker room and heard the news. "Well, where is Dennis so we can ask him?" Mary asked.

Wade began to look uncomfortable, glancing down the hall toward the office. "I don't know. Maybe he's in the office."

Sam, his jaw thrust out, said, "Why don't you ladies wait right here, and I'll go see if I can find him." He walked briskly down the hall toward the office.

The other regulars began to arrive, filtering out of the locker rooms singly and in pairs. Joe saw the gathering at the door. "What's going on?" he wanted to know.

Everyone began talking at once until finally Mary managed to tell what Wade had announced.

Joe turned to Wade. "What kind of maintenance?"

Wade looked more uncomfortable. "I don't really know. You'll have to ask Dennis."

George Riley stretched up to peer into the exercise room through the panel on the door. "It doesn't look like there's anyone in there working on anything. What's the story, Wade?"

At that moment Dennis came striding up the hall with Sam hurrying to try to keep up with him. Sam called out, "Wait'll you guys hear this scam. They're going to keep the exercise room shut until 12:10 so everyone can get a chance at the machines. How do you like those apples?"

There was a ripple of comments, and Joe cut through it, "It won't work, Dennis. The schedule clearly states the facilities will be open continuously on a first-come, first-served basis except for cleaning and maintenance. Now, is there some hazardous situation in there that the equipment can't be used? If not, you better move Wade and open up or you may have a breach of contract problem."

Dennis grimaced and waved Wade aside. The assembled Raiders trooped in and spread out at various stations. The comments about the attempt to keep them out were a mite caustic to say the least. A little later Dennis stopped by the treadmill Joe was using. "If you have the time Ms. Taylor wanted you to drop by the office later."

Joe decided not to make it too easy. "Why?"

"I guess she wants to talk to you."

"About what?"

Dennis' face was getting redder by the second, and he was biting at his mustache. "I don't really know, you'll have to ask her."

Joe said, "I'll think about it."

— • • • • • —

Joe left the exercise room about 12:20 and swam laps for twenty minutes before showering. Dressed and feeling refreshed he walked down the hall toward the office. Ms. Taylor was evidently watching for him and met him at the door.

"Mr. Rossi, I'm glad you decided to stop by. We need to talk. Please, have a seat."

He came into the office and sat in an arm chair opposite her desk. Ann Taylor was an attractive woman, late forties he guessed. Trim, fit, well-groomed. The perfect walking advertisement for a health club. The smile that never touched her eyes gave her face a hard, brittle look, he thought.

"So, what did you want to talk about, Ms. Taylor?"

The smile faded. "What is it you want, Mr. Rossi?"

He thought about that for a few moments and calmly answered, "I really don't want anything, Ms. Taylor."

The flash of annoyance was like a ripple of heat lightning, momentarily there and then gone. "Look, let's stop jousting and get this out in the open."

"Ms. Taylor, you requested this meeting. If you have something to say I suggest you do so."

"All right! What's it going to take to have you call off this conspiracy to tie up the exercise room at lunch time everyday?"

Joe frowned. "Conspiracy? Don't you think that sounds a little ridiculous?"

It was her turn to frown, and she leaned forward on the desk to emphasize her point, "Well, Mr. Rossi, for the past three weeks your people have assembled during the busiest usage period to tie up the equipment. That, in itself, looks planned."

Joe leaned back in his chair, calm and relaxed as he answered, "So?"

"So how about we come to some agreement? You, and some of the others, were very outspoken about having to take full membership in the club. Suppose we were prepared to allow everyone over age sixty to have limited pool membership again?" What she said was couched as a question but was really a proposal.

Joe waited, showing neither approval nor disapproval. "Ms. Taylor, you keep referring to my people. I can only answer for myself. If you want to know everyone else's decision you'll have to ask them."

"Come on, Mr. Rossi! How can I do that?"

Joe smiled amiably as he answered, "The same way you did it when you raised their membership rates: by mail. I'd just as soon keep my full membership. I kind of like the complete fitness approach. You'll have to ask the others yourself." He nodded politely to her as he left the office.

—•••••—

As Joe came into the Senior Center he was bombarded with questions about what went on in the meeting with the "Iron Maiden." He slipped off his coat and waited until they were ready to listen.

"Well, it worked. She's ready to let anyone who wants to, go back to a limited membership."

There was applause and cheers and laughter. "We stuck it to them, didn't we?" Sam chortled.

The queries from the group were a staccato burst of verbiage. Will there be a refund? How are we supposed to find out? When will it go into effect? Suppose we don't want to go back on limited?

This last question hung in the air as Joe held up his hands in token of surrender, grinning all the while. Finally, they were ready to let him speak.

"Look, I told her I wasn't the spokesman for anyone, that you all acted on your own. Please, don't make a liar out of me." A ripple of laughter accompanied the nods. "Ms. Taylor will make the offer to each of you by mail, and you all will have to decide what you want to do."

"Well hell! Isn't this what we all wanted, what we were all working for?" Sam growled, glowering around at the group.

There was a general shifting around in seats as they glanced about trying to gauge reactions. But no one answered him.

Joe turned to Sally Simon. "Sally, do you still have sore buns?"

There was a moment of stunned silence followed immediately by a wave of laughter.

Joe, red faced, hurriedly interjected, "No disrespect intended, Sally. I'm just trying to make a point."

"No, as a matter of fact, I feel pretty good, and I've lost three pounds," Sally answered, her own face showing more color.

Joe continued, "How about you, Marty? Are you sleeping well?"

"How can I tell, Joe. I'm asleep all night," Marty answered in mock, straight-faced innocence.

Helen Gordon piped in, "I've lost weight too. Not a lot, but it's a start."

"Me too!" Mary nodded. "And George's back hasn't been bothering him nearly as much either."

They looked around, one to the other, and began to smile. It was Frank Almond who summed it up, "It looks like we won the battle, and now most of us aren't sure we really want what we were fighting for in the first place."

Faye Almond, who rarely had much to say about anything in the group discussions, suddenly spoke up, to everyone's astonishment, "I think Joe is trying to tell us that we've all won something else. We've all come to the realization that we all feel better when we do regular workouts. None of us, not even Joe, wanted to do anything but swim a few laps. We forced ourselves to start exercising just to spite them and now we realize it's been good for us. Frank and I have been talking about it, and we've decided to keep the full membership."

"I'm keeping mine too," Joe added. "But everyone has to make his own decision."

Sam, chin thrust out aggressively, had been taking it all in and not saying anything, which for him was unusual. Finally, he rubbed his bald head vigorously and entered the discussion, "Hey, suppose we all decide to stay with the full membership. How about we push the 'Iron Maiden' for a senior discount. We should be able to convince her we could all rearrange our schedules so we don't use the equipment at lunch time. How about that?"

"Do you think we dare?" Helen asked.

Joe nodded and said, "Hell, yes! It's worth a try. It'll be a big savings over having to refund us all for a limited membership."

There was a flurry of comments and questions as the body of plan B began to take shape. Rossi's Raiders were beginning a new campaign.

Rainbow's End

"Don't touch her!"

"Well, hell! How else am I gonna get the oatmeal outta the pan if I don't pack it on her? You know she'll buck and kick like she always does when I pack loose pans on her. We ain't got enough water left to wash it out."

"That's why I say don't touch her. I packed the blasting caps on her, and if she starts up, we're liable to have pieces of mule scattered over three counties, you damn fool."

"Well, how was I to know, Jake. We ain't packed any dynamite or caps for years. I suppose the sticks are on Hamlet."

"You suppose right, and I don't want anything upsetting Ophelia. So you just let me lead her, and you take Hamlet."

"When we gonna get rid of these damn mules anyway? We got enough now to cash in and get us one of them four-by-four trucks that'll take us anywheres we want to go, in a lot less time. And they smell better than Hamlet and Ophelia."

"You got a helluva nerve, Lonnie. You don't smell none too sweet yourself. I expect that's why Ophelia acts up when she's around you."

"Shoot! I get wet every time we pan. What more do you want?"

"You might try some soap occasionally. And that shirt and jacket are a mite ripe by anybody's standards."

"Well, how about that idea about getting a jeep or something? We could turn old Hamlet and Ophelia out to pasture over in the National Park. They'd have lots of grazeland to wander and nobody to bother them."

"Look, Lonnie, right now we wander around these hills, sometimes on gov'ment land and sometimes on private property, and nobody bothers us. We're just two crazy old farts lookin' for gold. Nobody takes us serious. So we wander in to Redwood City and cash in sixty, seventy dollars in dust once in a while and blow it all on supplies. Ain't nobody knows what we got hidden away here and there. What'cha suppose they'd think if we cashed in enough dust to buy a jeep?"

Lonnie scratched his head and grimaced. He stared off over the tree tops and finally heaved a deep sigh. "I expect we'd have about a million people doggin' our every move to find out where the strike was."

"Exactly right! And all those ranchers and farmers who grin and wave at us would begin to wonder how much we took off'a their land. And all those Park Rangers would begin askin' how much we took off'a gov'ment land, too."

"How much you figure we got now, Jake? I mean all of it, in all the hidin' places?"

"I dunno, not for sure anyways. We got no scales. But that pocket we found in the park last year has to be worth seventy, maybe eighty thousand. Took us near a month to work that vein."

"Yeah, I know that, Jake, but how about the other stashes? How much all together?"

Jake scratched at his cheek through the beard and thought about it for a while before he answered, "I expect we got close to a quarter million dollars."

Lonnie whistled. "And we can't figure a way for cashin' it in without all hell bustin' loose. What're we gonna do, Jake? How we gonna' get it out?"

"I been thinkin' on it, and this is what I figure we can do. We work our way west fifty, sixty miles to that area that got hit by the floods. I heard on the portable, 'fore the batteries went dead, that folks are pannin' gold and even findin' small nuggets. They got a mini-rush goin' on right here in California." He rubbed his hand across his beard a few times and continued, "I don't figure nobody's gonna get too excited if we begins to cash in a thousand or two up and down the valley. They'll just figure we're luckier and more experienced than most.

"We split up and make like we don't know each other and with any kinda luck we can convince folks we found the stuff in the flood areas. You take Hamlet and I'll take Ophelia, and we'll meet back here at Dutchman's Knob in a month. And then we go back and do it all over again. You follow what I'm sayin', Lonnie?"

Lonnie was grinning and nodding as he listened to the plan. "How much are we gonna cash in, Jake?"

"Just enough to get us travelin' money. We'll buy us an old panel truck and take the rest out in boxes. We can turn Hamlet and Ophelia loose after our last trip."

"But how..."

"Shut up and listen, Lonnie. We make up small parcels and have 'em shipped UPS to San Diego to be held for pick-up. Then we drive down and pick 'em up."

"Then what, Jake?"

"Then, you damn fool, we slip it across the border in small packages. It'll mean a lot of trips back and forth, but what the hell, we got all the time in the world. When we got all our cash, we can fly to Brazil, or Switzerland, or wherever we damn well please."

Lonnie was looking a little awed as Jake's plan was unfolding. Finally he asked, "How'd you figure all this out anyways? I know you're smarter'n me, but not that much smarter."

"I got the idea from one of those paperback books you always rib me about. This detective story had the start of a plan like this, and another one or two gave me ideas for the rest of it. It should work if we're careful. You don't talk to nobody, Lonnie. Y'hear? And you stay away from the booze or you'll blow the whole plan to hell and gone. We've worked nigh on to six years puttin' this stash together. Gettin' careless now would be stupid. Right?"

"Right, Jake! Remember, I ain't been on the sauce since we started partners six years ago. The need's just ain't there no more. Like you said, we got too much to lose if I screw up."

"But what are we gonna do with the dynamite we got left?"

Jake grinned and said, "Well, we gotta go through the park. It's the shortest way. We'll just swing by that crumbly outcrop alongside where we found that pocket. If nobody's around, we'll give it a half stick shot, just to see if there's any more stuff underneath. If so, we'll stay and put the plan on the back burner for a spell. OK?"

Lonnie nodded, grinning broadly.

—• • ● • •—

The two grizzled, raggedy men led the mules down the rocky trail to a gravel road. A dusty pick-up truck approached and passed them, kicking up a cloud of dust. The driver tooted his horn, grinned and waved as he passed them. The two old timers waved back and continued to plod along, moving west.

Singular Choices

He couldn't, for the life of him, understand why he'd ever agreed to meet with her. What could come of it after all that had happened? It wasn't as if either of them had hinted at a reconciliation. So, he wondered, why had she called?

Brian Mullins was a questioner, who warily weighed and assessed the motives behind his own and everyone else's actions. He was deep into that pattern now as he drove toward Edgeton. Maybe it was his curiosity. Maybe he should be suspicious or at least on guard.

After all, the breakup hadn't been completely without some hurt feelings. He was thinking about the old cliché about a woman scorned. Well, it wasn't really like that; it was more like a mutual desire to end the relationship. Even now, deep down, he had the nagging feeling that it had been a mistake. He wondered if she had some of the same misgivings. It'd been just too damned easy to walk away from the marriage. He had to admit he'd been a little hurt even in the midst of his relief at it being over and done with. It was only natural, he supposed, that she'd have some similar feelings.

He drove along the interstate only vaguely aware of the traffic flow, his mind alive with a random array of memories of their time together. He found himself smiling at some and then allowed himself to switch his thoughts to the drabness that had seemed to close in to wring out the last of the feelings they'd shared. Once again he found himself asking if it was really his own shallowness, his reluctance to accept the commitment. He wondered just how close she'd come to the truth when she'd said, "It isn't just marriage, Brian, it's any hint of commitment that sends you scurrying to protect your independence." There were no concrete answers, he thought, only the questions that seemed to multiply in his mind.

Brian was suddenly aware he'd passed under a display of road signs stretched across the highway. He began to search hurriedly for landmarks to orientate himself. He was almost at the first interchange for Edgeton. He nudged his way into the right lane and signaled his intention to exit. He was there, and he wasn't sure he wanted to be.

As he pulled onto the Boulevard he glanced at his watch. He was early. That would never do; it would look as if he was eager. Suddenly he was angry with himself. Here he was reverting to the petty maneuvering of the past. Brian drove into the parking area alongside a cocktail lounge and debated whether or not to go in to kill some time. No need to be too late; that would create an atmosphere of confrontation. He didn't want to hurt her, just maintain his independence. Why, he asked himself, are you so damned touchy about your independence? He sat for a few more minutes and then drove out of the parking lot.

———•••••———

Her apartment was small and kind of dingy, he thought, but then the room and a half he had was no bargain either. He missed their old, clean apartment and all the niceties of regular laundry and hot meals, but he wasn't ready to admit it, even to himself. Most of all he missed the warmth of her, the sheer delight in their lovemaking... when they weren't arguing, that is.

He waited while she put up some coffee in the tiny kitchenette. Brian could see her standing at the counter, her back toward him, and he thought she looked thinner and a little drawn. Sharon turned and saw him watching her and started to smile but quickly caught herself. She came back into the room and sat opposite him. They both began to speak at the same time and then stopped to let the other continue. Then they both smiled and for that brief second it was as golden as it had ever been. Brian caught himself first and withdrew into his defensive shell. Her smile faded as she watched it happen, and she turned away to look out the window.

"I suppose you're wondering why I asked you to come. Before I say anything else, I want to thank you for coming. I know you didn't have to."

"That's right, I didn't have to."

"So, why did you?" There was a challenge in her tone.

"I don't know, I really don't. I guess I was curious. I couldn't imagine why we would need to see each other again. The breakup seemed final enough."

She nodded slowly as she thought about that. "You're right. We both said all the mean and nasty things we'd been saving for too long, and that was the end of it."

He didn't answer. He just sat there staring at her from behind his wall of indifference.

"I still can't get over how easy it was," she said. "We were both so passive, so ready to throw away... whatever it was we had to begin with." She paused and shook herself as if a sudden chill had passed over her.

"Look, Brian, I asked you to meet me because we have a problem... an unexpected problem."

He could feel himself getting wary, feverishly searching for some bit of unfinished business they'd both overlooked.

"I'm pregnant, Brian."

His eyes widened. A muscle in his jaw twitched. They stared at each other for a moment before he blurted, "That's just great! How the hell did that happen?"

"The usual way." She was maddingly calm. "It's only been six weeks since we were at the lake together. I'm sure you remember that long, passionate weekend that was supposed to make everything right for us again." There was no mistaking the note of sarcasm in her tone, and he reacted to it.

"Yeah, I remember. It seemed like a wonderful idea at the time. We took a trip to fantasy land. I think, deep down, we knew nothing was going to change for us... and it didn't." His bluntness was pure retaliation.

"Look, Brian, the only thing I'm asking from you is a little help, financially." She turned toward the window before she finished. "I'm going to have an abortion."

"An abortion!" Again his expression reflected his shock.

"It's the only way out of this. I need my job, now more than ever, and I can't raise a child alone. There isn't any way I can work and pay for child care... even if I wanted to."

He sat there shaking his head in disbelief.

"This way it will be over," she continued. "There won't be any ties, no child support or custody concerns or visitation rights. Nothing. Finished. Over and done with."

"Is that what you want? I mean, is that what we want?"

"What alternative do we have?"

"I don't know." He got up and walked to the window. He stood looking out, his back to the room. Finally he turned to face her. "Look, Sharon, I don't know what to say. You've hit me with this and I wasn't ready for it. Let me think about it a little. I'll call you."

"When?"

"Tomorrow, the day after, I don't know. Dammit, don't start pushing me."

It was her turn to be annoyed, and her tone reflected it. "I'm not pushing. It's just that I don't have a lot of time. I need to make some arrangements."

"Okay! I'll call you... no later than Tuesday."

——•••••—

Brian Mullins drove back down the interstate trying mightily to sort out his feelings. He was angry with Sharon, with himself, with the damned inevitability of the situation. She must be having a rough time of it, he thought, and he felt a little guilty. Why should he feel guilty? He wasn't the only one to blame, he thought. He turned off at the second Kelsoe exit and headed for the Tin Horse. Allen and Matt and the crowd were sure to be there watching football and arguing, as usual, and drinking beer. It was a Sunday ritual. Today was Sunday.

"Hey! Here comes Brian-o the wino!" Matt called as Brian walked into the bar.

Allen watched him cross the room to the group gathered around the TV. "You're late. Where you been, anyway?"

"I had to take a run up to Edgeton to see someone." He was feeling evasive.

Allen just smiled and took a pull at his beer. Brian could feel himself getting annoyed, but he kept his cool and remained silent.

Matt and Chuck were in a heated discussion about a pass interference call, and they watched the replay pointing out why the call was right or wrong. The routine was old. Brian had witnessed four or five variations of it at least fifty times... maybe more. He was aware of Allen watching him, and it was making him tense.

"What!" He was staring right into Allen's eyes as he said it, and he could feel his jaw tighten as he struggled for control.

"She just won't let it go, will she?" Allen was half smiling in that mocking way of his that Brian resented.

"Leave it alone, Allen. Just leave it alone. It's none of your business."

Brian had answered softly, but what he said, or maybe the way he said it, cut through the babble between Matt and Chuck and the noise of the TV. Suddenly there was silence accented by the game audio. Everyone turned to look at Brian. Vinnie, who was over by the bar sweet-talking some girl, stopped his routine to stare back over his shoulder.

Brian and Allen sat silently staring at each other across the table. Finally Allen said, "You're right, it's none of my business. You do whatever you want." The shadow of the smirking smile was there but not nearly so noticeable.

Vinnie wandered over from the bar with a fresh beer. "Hey, Brian, where you been, man? We thought you weren't coming. Be my guest, have a beer."

Brian took it and drank off a mouthful. He grinned at Vinnie and asked, "What's the score?"

"Redskins, ten to seven. They're looking good today."

Chuck laughed, "You wish."

And just as suddenly the tension was gone, and the babble started up again as if nothing had happened. Allen and Brian found ways not to talk to each other without it seeming too obvious.

Brian found himself looking from one to the other of the group, seeing them perhaps for the first time stripped of their facades, the macho image each of them worked so hard to project.

They were an ordinary bunch of guys tenaciously clinging to their youth even as it was slipping inescapably away. They were part of a larger group which formed a loosely knit pick-up league, ready to compete in everything from basketball to touch football to volleyball. The older, slower players were tolerated, just barely, mocked and teased by the younger guys. In a few years, he thought, we'll all be there, straining to keep up. He could picture the young studs laughing and making faces behind his back, and it didn't set well. Reaching thirty seemed to be the dreaded abyss from which there was no reprieve.

They all tried too damned hard, himself included, constantly competing with themselves and each other. Matt and Vinnie traded winning and losing at whatever they tried; they were that evenly matched. Klutzy Chuck tried to beat anyone at anything. It was a rainbow day for him when he succeeded.

Then there was Allen. Brian turned his chair a little to look at him. Allen was watching the game intently, completely absorbed. It was typical, he thought, the intensity in everything Allen did: his job, his play, his relationships. He smiled to himself remembering what Sharon had once said. "Allen isn't your friend," she had said, "he is your driver, your competitor." He'd laughed it off at the time, but it came back again and again as truth. Maybe they needed each other for the motivation they provided. The overpowering compulsion to win, to be the best, was an obsession neither of them could relinquish.

It had started with grades in college and points scored in basketball. Now it was sales, salary and career advancement. Brian was tired of it. The whole routine was old, but there didn't seem to be any way to end it. It was funny the way things happened. Allen had begun seeing Sharon, and they dated fairly steadily for a while. He couldn't remember when he'd become interested in Sharon. It must have been one of those times Allen and Sharon had stopped seeing each other. That happened at least twice he could remember. At first he dated Sharon just to get to Allen, and he was pretty sure it was her reason, too. He never meant for it to turn serious, but it did. Was he in love with her then or was it an extension of the rivalry? Did he really want to marry Sharon, or just keep Allen from doing so? He tried to put it out of his mind. It wasn't something he was comfortable with. Was he in love with her now? That was even more unsettling to think about.

Brian got up from his seat and walked to the front of the bar. Everyone was engrossed in the game and hardly noticed as he pulled on his windbreaker and left. It was snowing lightly, soft, tiny flakes hardly discernible except against the darker buildings along the street. He walked past the lot where his car was parked and on up the street. The air was crisp; he could hardly feel the snow touching his face. He lost track of time as he walked, weighing the decisions he'd made, the choices that had shaped his life, trying to imagine where he'd be five years from now, or even one year from now. Suddenly he was aware of the gathering dusk. It wasn't snowing any harder, and the streets were hardly even wet. He glanced at his watch, 4:10. He turned toward a bank of phones and fumbled in his pocket for change. She answered on the second ring.

"Sharon, it's me, Brian. I need to talk to you."

There was silence for a few seconds before she answered, "Tonight?"

"Yeah, tonight, if that's okay."

"Brian, it's snowing here. Do you want to come all that way? Can't it wait?"

"Not really. Besides the snow's not going to amount to anything."

"Have you had supper? I'm just making spaghetti. Shall I put some in for you?"

"That would be great. I'll see you in a little while."

"Be careful, the roads may be slick."

He hung up the phone and stood looking at it. He felt good about her response: have you had supper? Be careful! Suddenly a sense of sadness came over him as he walked back to the car, and he made no effort to rationalize it.

——•••••——

Brian sat in the same chair he'd sat in earlier in the day. He was wearing his windbreaker and the melted snow in his hair glistened in the light from the lamp alongside his chair. Sharon stood leaning against the door jamb of the kitchenette. He thought her expression, even the way she stood with her arms folded about herself, was questioning. And he didn't know what to say, or how to begin. He felt awkward and unsure. There was so much he wanted to say, but it all seemed an unintelligible jumble in his mind. He could hear the traffic in the street outside, the unmistakable sound tires make on wet pavement. Sharon tilted her head a little as she waited, but her quizzical expression never changed.

Finally, he blurted it out, "I don't want us to get a divorce."

The quizzical look turned to one of resignation, and she shook her head slowly.

"Please, Sharon, just hear me out. I've had a whole lot of time to think about us since we broke up. Not too much of it made sense until today."

"Oh Brian, what's the use. We've been over this so many times, and nothing ever changes." She had come into the room and sat on the couch across from him. There was no mistaking the weariness in her voice.

"I love you, Sharon. I just didn't know it. I was too busy with my own agenda — what I selfishly wanted out of life and of course my independence." He paused, groping for the right words, surprised at his own honesty. He wasn't holding back, hedging what he had to say to ensure his chances of getting out of it if he felt he had to. It was a new experience.

"I love you too, Brian, but I don't like you." It was said simply, a statement of fact said without rancor.

"I took a good look at myself today, for the first time in a long time, and I didn't like what I saw either."

"What do you want me to say, Brian? We were pretty thorough the last time we inventoried each other's faults."

"Yeah, I know. Maybe too much so. But at least it forced me to think about us, about myself and my priorities. I have to honestly say I don't know if I was in love with you when we were married. I'm not proud of having to admit that, but I needed to get it out in the open."

Sharon kicked off her loafers and tucked her legs and feet alongside her on the couch. She found herself wanting to listen to what he had to say. It was so out of character for Brian to admit to anything, especially his own feelings.

"I thought I was in love with you. I honestly did. But I think I'm beginning to realize I didn't know what I was feeling then. It's only since we've been apart these last weeks that I've come to actually realize what we've lost. Or maybe I should say what I threw away with my stubborn, selfish attitude."

"Are you sure this isn't about what I told you earlier today? You aren't confusing guilt, or pity, or compassion with love, are you, Brian?"

"No." His voice was quiet, controlled, "That's not what's happening at all. I've known, almost from the beginning, that the breakup wasn't right for us. I've been too pig-headed to admit it, even to myself. You, better than anyone, must know how hard it is for me to admit I'm wrong... about anything."

She laughed. It was spontaneous and held no hint of accusation. His refusal to ever admit he was wrong had been the source of many of their troubles. He watched her for a moment, then his earnest expression relaxed into a smile.

"I don't want to sound like I'm trying to blame someone else for my actions." He paused, choosing his words carefully. "But hanging out with Allen and Vinnie and that crowd hasn't helped me accept being married."

"What are you getting at? What's all this leading up to?"

"I told you right at the beginning: I don't want us to get a divorce."

"Too much has happened for us to just pick up where we left off." There was a note of sadness in her voice, a note of resignation that was a message in itself. "Are you sure you know what you're getting into? Honestly, Brian, I'm not sure at this point you're ready to be a husband, much less a father. The novelty of a baby will wear off fast," she paused and put her head down, "just the way our being together did."

Brian got out of his chair and went to sit facing her on the opposite end of the couch. "I know it sounds crazy, especially in light of what's happened, but you've got to give me — us — a chance. I know we can't start over again as if none of it ever happened. Please, let me come to see you. Let's get to know each other, maybe in a way we never did before." His seriousness was disconcerting, and she felt confused and defensive.

"Let me prove I really care about us." He grinned, "Maybe I can even get to be likable."

"I'm almost six weeks pregnant, Brian. We don't have time for this." There was no mistaking the concern in her voice. "Maybe we could make it work, but I can't afford to gamble on it. I have too much to lose."

"What about what I have to lose? I could lose you and the baby, both. Isn't that worth a gamble?" He waited for her to answer and when she hesitated he added, "You said before that you loved me. Let me prove to you that I really do love you."

"How are we going to do that in the time we have left? The doctor at the clinic said the... you know... the procedure is fairly simple during the first trimester. After that, it could get complicated. I just don't know, Brian."

"Will you give me the time that's left to convince you? No, give me three weeks, and then if you want to go through with it, I'll help you any way you want me to."

Sharon rose from the couch and walked to the window. She was close to tears and didn't want him to know it. She was trying hard not to let herself believe what he was saying. Finally, she turned to face him.

"All right, Brian. I'll wait the three weeks, and you can come visit if you like, but nothing has really changed as far as I'm concerned. You won't be able to quit hanging out with Allen and the others. Even if you try, they won't leave you alone. The urge to play a little basketball, or go to the games, or just hang out will take over again. And I'm not ready to be totally shut out of your life the way it was before." She wasn't able to hold back the tears, and she was angry about that.

"It'll be different this time, Sharon. I promise."

"Prove it, Brian! Go ahead, prove it! Convince me it will be different."

—•••••—

Brian Mullins glanced at his watch as he entered the terminal. He was early. Traffic on the way to the airport had been surprisingly light, and now he had fifty minutes to kill before arrival time. He checked one of the monitors to be sure the flight was on time, and then he decided to pick up something to read and have some coffee. He bought a copy of *USA TODAY* and walked into the coffee shop. He sat halfway down the counter and began to read the lead story. The waitress refilled his cup as he was turning to another section when he felt a hand on his shoulder.

"Hello, Brian."

He turned, but he knew the voice even before their eyes met. "Hello, Allen. What are you doing in Edgeton?"

"I've been here a few days on business. I'm just on my way back to Dallas."

"So how's the new job going? Last I heard from Matt, or maybe it was Chuck, you were thinking about a job offer in California."

"Yeah, I had an offer, but I decided against it. I'm with a good company, and I think I'm making a contribution. They seem to like what I'm doing for them, and that's a big plus. Do you see much of the old crowd?"

Brian had folded the paper and risen from the stool, groping for some money to leave for the coffee and the tip. "Yeah, some of us go out for a couple of beers once in a while, but nothing regular. Everyone's so busy. I guess you heard Vinnie got married. You remember the redhead he went out with a year or so ago? You know, the lady firefighter? That was a real surprise. Matt just got engaged to someone who transferred into his company from Illinois or someplace. We haven't met her yet, but Chuck says she is a very pretty lady. How about you, Allen? Are you involved with anyone?"

"I really don't have the time, Brian. The job and the travel take a lot of my time. I date some," he shrugged, "but nothing serious. How's Sharon?"

"She's fine. She's coming in from Milwaukee in about twenty minutes. She spent a week with her parents. They saw the baby right after she was born, but not since then."

"How old is the baby now?"

"Sandra is almost a year old and looks just like Sharon. Man, I don't know where the time goes. She's crawling and about ready to walk, I think. Hey, when's your plane leaving? Maybe you'd like to say hello to Sharon and see the baby?"

Allen glanced at his watch and shook his head. "I wish I could but I have an important call to make, and that will take me right up to boarding time. Say hello to Sharon for me. Maybe I'll give you a call next time I'm in town."

"That would be great. Hey, we live in Hermitage now. Our number's in the book."

Allen waved as he walked briskly out of the coffee shop into the pedestrian crush of the terminal mall. Brian watched him go, knowing he wouldn't ever call and feeling a little satisfied about that.

The public address system announced flight 122 from Milwaukee arriving at gate eleven. Brian walked into the terminal mall and turned toward the arrival gates, suddenly amazed at his own contentment with his life.

Talk

"Hello, Mildred? This is Eunice. I'm sorry to be calling so early, but I thought you'd like to know who Duane saw in Kelsoe yesterday." She paused, smiling as she listened, and then nodded as she continued, "Well, you see Duane drove over to Kelsoe to pick up some things I ordered from the Penney's catalog and guess who he saw going into that Women's Free Clinic over on Landry Street? Well, it was that new Miss Ramey, that's who. It struck him odd her going in there. That clinic, I hear tell, specializes in women's ailments, including pregnancy and such. There's talk she's divorced. She's not married now, is she?"

She listened intently for a few moments, nodding and smiling to herself and then answered. "I didn't think so. Well, anyway, I thought you ought to know. After all, she is Billy Joe's teacher this year, ain't she?"

—•••••—

Duane Suggs sat on the loading dock with Willie and Slim and Bull Peters rooting through the debris in his lunch box, looking for the cigarettes Eunice usually packed for him. He opened up the pack and lit up.

"I was real surprised to see her going into that clinic building here in Kelsoe. Hell, I say if she was sick how come she couldn't go to a doctor back in Hermitage, where she lives, instead of coming all the way here to Kelsoe. I wonder what the big secret is?" He grinned as he glanced around at the others.

Bull Peters took a long pull on his can of Dr. Pepper and snorted, "What did you expect, bringing a 'de-vor-see' in here from the city. That new school superintendent has got some strange ideas. Don't know about you guys, but I hear there's some strange goings on at that 'country club' high school. Just you figure it out for yourself; anybody stacked like she is, is bound to get some serious attention from somebody." He leered at them, "If you know what I mean."

There was a round of ribald laughter coupled with some equally ribald comments about the physical attributes of Linda Ramey and her activities. Slim Brolly offered a thought which opened a whole new avenue of sordid speculation when he said, "Hey! You don't suppose that hot-shot superintendent brought her in here for his own private stock, do you? Man, rank sure has its privileges, don't it."

Duane piped in again, not willing to give up his place as the center of attention, "Eunice says she's kin to Mike Ramey, the cop. She's his sister and stayed with them until she got hired at school and found an apartment."

"So, she's got her own apartment," Slim said. "That ought to make it convenient for a little private screwing around. How about it, Bull, would you kick her out of bed?"

Bull grunted and said, "What the hell do you think?" And there was laughter and whistles and clapping from the group.

— • • • • • —

Pete's Tavern was only a few short blocks from the plant, which made it the watering hole of choice for most of the plant workers at the end of shift. There was a fair-sized crowd clustered along the bar and spread out into the seven or eight booths along the opposite wall. Pete Micelli and his wife Rosalie were busily drawing beers and bustling back and forth serving the crush at the bar. Marie was late, so Rosalie was carrying trays of beer to the men in the booths, bitching and complaining all the while.

Marie came in looking hot and harried. She disappeared into the back and came out almost immediately tying on an apron. Rosalie glared at her but didn't say anything.

"The baby has a fever. I had to wait for my sister."

"Where's Luther?" Rosalie wanted to know.

"Who the hell knows? I sure don't." Marie took the tray and shouldered her way through the crowd at the bar. Slim Brolly reached out and grabbed a feel as she went by and then tried to look innocently in the other direction.

"You're going to get a kick in the nuts some day soon, Slim," she said over her shoulder, still moving toward the bar.

"What? What's your problem, Marie?" Slim wanted to know, flashing a slack-mouthed grin.

Marie never answered, but Pete gave old Slim a look that offered trouble, and Slim shrugged and shook his head.

Walt Williams came into the bar and stood looking through the raucous crowd milling about. Walt Williams was a sometimes club fighter, mostly retired now, broad of shoulders and going to fat. He still thought of himself as a tough dude, and Mildred had the bruises to prove it. There were half a dozen men grouped below the TV mounted over the bar, arguing over the merits of the pitching in the ball game. He spotted Duane and Slim, but Bull Peters was not in the crowd. He paid Rosalie for a beer and started toward the group by the TV. Duane saw him first and came toward him.

"Hey, Walt, how's it going?"

"OK, I guess, you know, same old shit." Walt drank off some of his beer and belched. "My old lady said Eunice called. Said you saw that new teacher here in Kelsoe going into some clinic."

"Yeah! Just strutting up the walk wiggling that nice ass of hers, big as life."

"She does have a nice ass, don't she, and a nice set of boobs, too, as I remember it from back-to-school night. My old lady talked me into going that night, I'm happy to say." He grinned and waved his empty glass at Marie as she passed. "You don't suppose she's knocked up, do you? I hear tell she's divorced."

Duane leaned forward to whisper confidentially, and Walt reared back. "Jesus, Duane, you stink! Man, do you ever need a shower. You need to tell me something, just say it. Don't crowd in on me, I can't take the smell."

Duane acted like his feelings were hurt. "Hell, Walt, I just came off shift. I can't help it if I perspire a lot."

"Nice, young, sweet things perspire, Duane. You and me, we sweat."

"OK! OK! What I was trying to say was maybe she was going there to arrange for an abortion. Maybe she's knocked up and don't want it, you know."

Walt and Duane were standing about three feet from one of the crowded booths. Marcus Cheatham, sitting on the end, caught some of the conversation, enough to know who and what they were talking about. Crystal Cheatham was outraged when he told her after supper. She'd been nagging at him about stopping at Pete's after work. She didn't approve of drinking — or much else for that matter. Marcus offered her the tidbit of gossip to get her mind off his having a few beers after work.

They'd been sitting on the porch watching the kids romping with the dog. She'd just finished yelling at the kids, "You two stay out of that tall grass or I'll be picking ticks off of you and that dog for the next week. You hear?"

"Yes, Mama."

Now she was building a head of steam as she digested the news Marcus had just offered.

Tomorrow she was going to talk with Reverend Alabaster about this. And about how the schools were just going down. It was the devil's doing, that's what. Now, more than ever, they needed to have a good Christian school for the children. It was something she'd been talking about for years.

—•••••—

Linda Ramey took the seat opposite Dr. Stark. The summons to meet with the superintendent did not surprise her; after all she was a new teacher. She was still a little apprehensive. She sat quietly waiting for him to look up from the folder he was reading. He was a relatively young man, early forties she guessed, slim, slightly built with a receding hair line.

Linda read again from the nameplate facing her on the front of his desk: Dr. Arthur L. Stark, Superintendent of Schools. She wondered what the L stood for. At that point he looked up and smiled.

"Do you mind waiting while I take a few moments to review your personnel file?"

She shook her head, "Not at all."

He turned back to the folder: Linda Wagner, maiden name Ramey, age 32, divorced, no children. Last employment Pittsburg, Pa. public schools, English Dept., nine years experience, excellent academic credentials, solid recommendations. Finally he looked up and began to speak.

"Ms. Ramey, when I first interviewed you last spring I could not imagine why you would want to move to a small city system. As I remember it, you said you were disenchanted with the urban environment. And, of course, the change in your personal life made a relocation desirable. You said you wanted to try a slower, quieter way of life, as I remember. You also said you have family here?"

"Yes, my brother and his family live here in Hermitage. He's a police officer."

He nodded and continued, "I warned you then that small town living could be very confining, certainly a far cry from the personal privacy you knew in the city."

"Dr. Stark, please, let's get to the point. What are you trying to tell me? Is there some problem with my teaching?"

He sighed and rocked back in his chair, almost reluctant to proceed. "Ms. Ramey, there's been talk — rumors really — that you are pregnant and are planning to have an abortion."

The silence closed in on them as they sat staring at each other across the desk. The muted buzz of the digital desk clock as the minute display changed finally broke the spell.

Linda's voice was calm and steady enough, but it was obvious she was shocked and upset.

"Dr. Stark, this is ridiculous! How in the world could such a story ever get started? I assure you I have done nothing to warrant such malicious gossip."

"Please understand, Ms. Ramey, no one is accusing you of any sort of misconduct. And I agree your privacy should be respected." He hesitated, "If that is at all possible in this town."

He shifted around uneasily in his chair and continued, "However, please understand I need some, ah – clarification. Certain circumstances have been brought to the attention of some individual board members."

"What circumstances? What are you talking about?"

"Well, one of your colleagues on staff mentioned you were sick at school one day recently. She heard you being sick in the lavatory of the women's teacher's room."

Linda started to reply, but he held up his hand and said, "Please, let me restate all the unsubstantiated rumors before you answer."

He glanced down at some penciled notes and continued, "Then it was reported that you were seen in Kelsoe on a recent Saturday morning sneaking," he held up his hands to indicate quotation marks, "into the new medical center on Landry Street. There is speculation that it is an abortion clinic. And, finally, your request for a personal leave came through the Board office. That seemed to confirm, at least in the minds of the rumor mongers, that all the talk was true."

Linda Ramey looked puzzled for a few moments and then began to laugh. It came over her in waves until Dr. Stark began to fear the onset of hysteria. Linda finally managed to control her laughter. Wiping tears from her eyes she responded, "I assure you that I am not pregnant. Unless pregnancy can now be caused by an air borne virus!"

Dr. Stark's eyes widened momentarily, and then he smiled, visibly at ease. Linda continued, "With regard to my being ill at school, that happened about 2:15 or so in the afternoon. I've always heard it described as morning sickness. But if you check the dates you will find it was the day the cafeteria served some tainted milk. A number of the students became ill, and some others on staff as well. The school nurse can verify all this, I'm sure."

Now the Superintendent rocked back in his chair shaking his head in disbelief, "I'm really sorry." But she interrupted him, "As for the trip to Kelsoe, I admit I was there. I did not sneak in as reported. I walked openly into the front entrance. I was there to interview for a part-time position as receptionist. You are aware that my salary here is considerably lower than it was in Pittsburg. Frankly, I need the extra income.

"The Women's Free Clinic is a new service offered by the local medical community to poor working women. They have hours two evenings a week and on Saturday to accommodate those women who can't get time off without loss of pay. And for the record, the clinic does not perform abortions."

"Ms. Ramey, I'm sorry any of this had to come up, but you do understand my position in relation to the board members. I really didn't have much choice regarding this matter."

"I understand completely, Dr. Stark, and there are no hard feelings on my part. I surely hope this will not create a negative atmosphere for me in the school system."

"This whole affair will be fully rectified. And please don't judge the whole town by this incident. There are many good and caring people here as you will come to know. You're new here, and folks are just curious. In a little while something or someone else will arouse their curiosity, and all this will be forgotten. The gossips will always be there. We mustn't let them prevail." He seemed sincere in his effort to make amends, and Linda was grateful.

She rose to go and hesitated as if deciding to add something. When she did speak it was softly with a note of urgency, "I've tried to keep my personal business as private as possible. That was why I offered no explanation on the form requesting the personal day. I must appear in Pittsburg to sign papers finalizing the divorce and the property settlement. It means flying out of Edgeton on Saturday and catching a return flight on Monday evening. There was no other way without taking additional time off. I do hope you can leave me some degree of privacy in this."

"The contract stipulates that personal days are personal and do not require an explanation if the individual chooses not to offer one. There is no reason for me to discuss this with anyone. This whole meeting is a personnel matter and will go no further than those Board members who requested my inquiry. There will be no public discussion of anything we've spoken about in confidence. Please, don't let yourself be provoked into any confrontational episodes with either parents or colleagues."

Linda Ramey settled into her teaching duties under the watchful scrutiny of a hard core of parents and co-workers who considered themselves the guardians of the community. As predicted by Dr. Stark, Linda Ramey was soon forgotten as word got out of an illicit affair involving one of the women at the plant and her supervisor.

Getting Even

It felt like a hangover — the worst possible hangover he could remember. The pain washed over him as he opened his eyes and tried to focus. Someone hovered over him and said, "Don't try to move for a while, you've had a concussion."

He blinked, trying to will away the pain, and was finally able to bring the nurse's face into focus. Middle-aged, fiftyish, he really didn't care. He felt something touch his lips. He accepted the straw and hungrily took a few sips of water. He wanted more, but she took it away.

"What happened?"

"You were in an accident. The deputy said you probably fell asleep. You drove into a bridge abutment."

"What else besides the concussion? I mean what other injuries do I have? How badly am I hurt?"

"You were very lucky. You do have an assortment of bruises and contusions. You are going to be in pain for some time, but you'll survive. The concussion was the worst of it, and that will take the longest to mend. You'd better try to sleep now, if you can."

He thought about that. Well, you did a pretty good job of it, probably totaled the car. He drifted off to sleep, and the headache became a huge kettle drum being pounded in his subconscious. Suddenly he was in a darkening woods wandering along a path that wound in and out among gnarled and twisted trees, and there she was standing in the path ahead of him. She was smiling slightly, that little half smile that always meant trouble. She raised her arm, pointed at him and began to laugh. He turned and ran down the path, the woods growing darker and the laughter following after him. He awakened with a start, and the pain enveloped him in waves of nausea. His heart was pounding, and he was hyperventilating. He laid there rigid, fighting the nausea and the pain, afraid to allow himself to sleep again. Afraid she would be there.

He hated her, hated her for the humiliation of his breakdown, the nastiness of the divorce. He'd promised himself during the long months of his recovery that he'd get even, make her pay. He drifted in and out of sleep savoring that thought.

— • • • • • —

Roger Nolen drove the rental car into Woodstowne just before noon and parked right in front of the Woodstowne Hotel. It was an old wooden building with a long porch and a row of rocking chairs. He felt stiff and sore and the nagging headache was never more than a whisper away. He'd checked himself out of the hospital in Whitelock against the advice of the doctors there. The bruises on his face had faded except for a smudge beneath his right eye. His glasses masked it to some extent, but it was still noticeable. His knees ached as he got out of the car. He tried hard not to limp as he climbed the short stairs to the porch. Roger could see a man watching from the window as he entered the lobby.

"Well now, you must be Mr. Nolen. Is that right?"

"That's right. I called from Whitelock to reserve a room for a few days."

"Well, my name's Tackett." He placed the registration card and a pen on the counter and watched as Roger Nolen filled it out and laid down the pen.

"I see you didn't fill in the company you work for, Mr. Nolen. Any reason for that?"

"I'm self employed, Mr. Tackett. Now, if you'll show me to my room I'd like to get settled in."

Tackett placed a key on the counter and said, "Just up the stairs to the right, Mr. Nolen. If you'll leave your keys I'll have Charley park your car in the lot and bring up your luggage." He paused and added, "You're looking poorly, Mr. Nolen. Are you feeling all right?"

Roger could feel himself getting annoyed and tried to dampen it. No need to create problems, he thought, just play it carefully.

"I've been in an accident. Just about totaled my car but luckily my injuries weren't serious. It'll take a few weeks for the aches and pains to go away, I guess."

Mr. Tackett was a portly man, big of belly and behind, with narrow shoulders and spindly legs that looked like they could barely support his weight. His face was ruddy, with piercing blue eyes, a heavy hooked nose and a tiny mouth. Roger thought he looked like a big, gray topped macaw. He shook his head slowly and muttered, "Too bad, too bad. Sorry to hear it. Hope you feel better soon."

— • • ● • • —

Roger got up off the bed and walked to the bathroom. He stared into the mirror at the fading bruises and wondered if he had succeeded in covering his tracks. He could only wait and see what developed. He wanted to call Joe Spencer, but he decided to wait another day to avoid suspicion. He hadn't slept well but at least there were no dreams. That was a plus.

Breakfast in the coffee shop was almost as dreary as dinner had been the night before. But he didn't feel up to searching out a restaurant. Woodstowne was obviously an overnight stop for salesmen and truckers and a market town for the surrounding farms, and not much else.

Back in the room he sat in the chintz-covered easy chair by the window and stared out at the brick storefronts across the street. The largest one was three stories and had ornate cornices and fancy brickwork around the windows. A granite square just below the roofline read: Brady Building-1902. The letters and numbers were dark metal, and stain marks had dribbled off them to mar the stone. He could see the hills and mountains behind the buildings, hazy and blue in the morning sun.

He needed to make some effort to make it appear he intended to stay, to establish residence. He chose Bratton Realtors from the list of agents in the yellow pages of the ridiculously skinny phone book. Roger was sure old Tackett, or someone else, listened in on his call to Bratton, and he made a mental note of it.

— • • ● • • —

It was a steal at two hundred a month. He had an uneasy feeling that there had to be something wrong with the place. A furnished house, even in Woodstowne, had to be worth more than that, he thought. Granted, it was small and it certainly wasn't in the best condition. The furniture was early attic, nothing matched, just a hodgepodge mixture of mismatched junk. But it was still a find. He kept walking through the place trying to find some tangible reason for the low rent. Mrs. Bratton waited in the living room. She didn't have much to say about the place except that it was owned by an elderly widow.

"If I decide to take it, how soon would you need to know?" he asked.

"I would appreciate it if you called me as soon as you decide," she said. "I may have someone else who wants to look at it, and I don't want to have a conflict."

Roger had his doubts. The house smelled musty and unlived in, but he nodded, "I'll call you as soon as I decide. Do you have anything else I might be able to see?"

"Not furnished, and not in this price range."

"Well, I need to make a few phone calls before I can make a decision. I'll be in touch as soon as I can."

He followed her out onto the small porch and waited for her to lock the door. She continued down the steps toward her car. She turned to see him waiting on the steps and said, "No need to lock up; no one bothers to come out here."

Mrs. Bratton was a dumpy-looking woman in her forties, or even fifties. It was hard to tell. She had wispy, grayish hair and a bland, expressionless face. For some strange reason he remembered his father's description of someone who could have been Mrs. Bratton's double.

Dad had described her as having thin blood, watery eyes, a pinched soul and hair the color of a mouse's tit. Roger would have added the personality of a wet Kleenex.

She dropped him at the hotel, and he assured her he would call within the next few days, probably sooner. He watched her drive away wondering what it was about her, or the house, or both that left him with an uneasy feeling. As he turned he could see Tackett taking it all in from the front window. He walked across the porch and into the lobby.

"I see Mrs. Bratton was showing you around. You looking for a place to stay?" he asked.

"I might be. I haven't decided yet." He was annoyed and wary. Too many questions from the old bastard, he thought.

"Well, I'm sure she took you out to the old Lipscomb place." He laughed a tinny, irritating little laugh. "She's forever having people move in and out of that place. And it's no wonder, after what happened there."

Roger had already taken his key and started up the stairs, but Tackett kept right on talking.

"A little house on the edge of the woods about a mile out of town."

Roger turned on the stairs to look back, and Tackett was looking up at him, a tiny grin lifting the corners of his tiny mouth. He could feel the anger welling up, but he held it in check. No need to let old nosy rattle him. Keep calm, follow the game plan. He nodded and grinned at Tackett as he continued up the stairs and let himself into his room. Suddenly he was exhausted and getting a headache. He stretched out on the bed and slept. He dreamt again that he was running through darkening woods with the sound of laughter, Martha's laughter, getting closer and closer. He writhed in his sleep, his thin body thrashing about, the thinning sandy hair tousled as he mumbled and shook his head. He awakened with a start, sweaty and breathing heavily. He felt old and tired and frightened. His head throbbed, his eyes felt gritty and he was cold.

What happened? He had to know. The waiting was beginning to get to him. There wasn't much chance she could have made it. He'd watched her car swerve back and forth across the road as she tried to regain control, and then it flipped all the way over and landed right side up. He'd watched it roll to a stop, rear wheels on the pavement, the front end pointed down the slope toward the ravine. He really hadn't bumped her that hard, just a sideswiping nudge. It must have been the rate of speed, he thought. He was doing over seventy just to bring his car alongside hers. For a moment he thought it might be hung up and he might have to push it over the edge. Then it began to move, slowly at first, but gathering speed as it rolled over the edge and down the steep slope.

Roger could hear the crashing of breaking branches as the car hurtled down the bank. There was a louder crash as it struck something solid, and then silence. He waited for an explosion or the glow of flames but there was none. He'd been nervously watching for traffic, but the road was deserted. He decided against trying to work his way down the slope on foot. Too many things could go wrong in the dark. Someone was sure to remember seeing his car pulled off the road under the trees. It was time to go.

He turned west toward the interstate and then north. Roger had to be back at the Holiday Inn in Brandon before dawn. One hundred twenty some miles in three and a half hours should pose no problems. He arrived in Brandon a little before five and drove down to the end of the string of rooms with entrances from the parking area. No one was around as he let himself into his room. He slept until his wake-up call at eight. He showered, shaved and had breakfast before checking out.

Trouble was, he was exhausted, mentally as well as physically. He planned all along to scrape his car on a tree or something to account for the damage done when he deliberately sideswiped Martha's car. The concrete bridge abutment seemed like the perfect spot but he miscalculated, most likely because he was so tired. The accident at the bridge had literally wiped out the whole right side of his car, twisting the frame beyond salvage and slamming him around inside the car.

Now, here he sat in Woodstowne after three days in the hospital and another day here. He decided it was safe to call Joe Spencer, but he wouldn't call from his room. There was an outdoor phone booth a little way up Main Street, and he decided to call from there. He punched in the number and waited for the call to go through. Looking back toward the hotel he could see Tackett watching from the front window. There wasn't much the old bastard missed.

"Spencer and Cole, good afternoon."

"Hello, this is Roger Nolen. I'm calling long distance for Mr. Spencer."

"May I tell him who's calling?"

"The name is Nolen, Roger Nolen." He spoke slowly, enunciating carefully, sarcastically.

"Please hold." He waited, and in a few moments Joe Spencer came on the line.

"Roger, where are you? I've been trying to reach you for the past two days." There was a note of urgency in his voice.

"I'm upstate, a little place called Woodstowne. I needed to get away for a while. Why were you trying to get me?"

There was a pause and then he answered, "Martha's missing."

"What do you mean, missing?"

"Martha went out to dinner with some friends Friday and they ended up at The Embers. She left there alone, sometime around one AM, and no one has seen her since. Her sister reported her missing on Sunday."

"Look, Joe, I don't give a damn about her or where she's gone. She's probably off on a trip somewhere, without bothering to tell anyone. It's typical. She'll call from Florida or somewhere when she's ready."

There was silence and Roger continued, "I gave up the apartment, Joe. I've rented a house up here. I'm going to try to write again. I've got to get myself back together."

There was a few moments of silence, and then Joe said, "The State Police found her car at the bottom of a ravine pretty badly wrecked. They don't think anyone could have survived the crash but there wasn't anyone in it."

"What are you telling me, Joe?"

"They don't know if Martha was driving or someone else was. They do know she was in the car. They found her handbag and one of her shoes. They searched the whole area for a mile or so and found nothing."

Roger leaned against the side of the phone booth. He felt weak and his head was beginning to ache again. He tried to control his breathing so his voice would sound calm and rational. "Joe, I had an accident on the way up here. I fell asleep at the wheel and hit a concrete abutment. I'm okay. I had a mild concussion and an assortment of bruises, but I'm okay."

He really wasn't okay. His head was pounding, and he felt nauseous. The rest of the conversation was a blur, about staying in touch and so forth. He couldn't wait for it to end. He needed some time to think.

He hung up the phone and stood there, his mind racing. What happened? Where did she get to? He knew she was in the car. He saw her slumped over the wheel while the car teetered on the edge of the ravine. Who moved the body? Could she have survived? He knew she recognized him in the split second before the crash. Suddenly he looked up to see Tackett staring at him from the window of the hotel. Someone was tapping on the door of the phone booth asking if he was all right.

—•••••—

It was early evening and dusk softened the surrounding trees as he pulled into the shallow drive alongside the cottage. A brisk wind had come up, and the trees rustled and swayed as he unloaded his few belongings and sacks of groceries he'd bought on his way out of town.

Roger was agitated. He had tried mightily to conceal it from Tackett without much success. Tackett asked twice if anything was wrong in the brief time it took to pay his bill. His denials only seemed to heighten Tackett's curiosity. Now he was so nervous he could only pace from room to room in the tiny house, wondering all the while what had happened.

Was she alive? How could that be? He was sure he saw her slumped over the wheel. Where was she? Had she somehow followed him? Did she know where he was? Damn her to hell! He stopped every so often to peer out the small picture window to the empty road in the gathering darkness. Finally he sat in a rickety rocker. There were no lights on in the house as he sat and stared at the darkening window. If only his head would stop pounding. He watched as a car went by slowly, headlights reflecting off the trees as it followed the curve of the road. A little while later the same car went by in the opposite direction. He was sure it was the same car.

The wind had picked up, and it whistled around the tiny house and created a roaring sound in the trees. Roger was frightened, his head ached and he began to shiver, even though it was not cold in that dark room. He listened to the wind; the sound seemed to change in pitch. He strained to hear something in the background, a different sound, almost like laughter, but it died away, lost in the wind.

Suddenly the flash of headlights raked the window as a car pulled into the short drive behind his rental car. A woman got out and stood alongside the car staring at the dark house.

Startled, Roger jumped up from the rocker in a near panic. He hurried through the house bumping into furniture and doorjambs as he fumbled his way to the back door. He rushed through the door, and it slammed shut behind him. The wind was roaring in the treetops. He couldn't decide what to do. His head was pounding, and he was frightened. Who was this woman? It couldn't be Martha, but.... He moved away from the house and into the trees. The moon was rising and there was a pale glow beginning to brighten the area.

Scudding clouds created the illusion of lights being raised and lowered in a ghostly way. The wind rose and fell; he turned his head to listen. It was there, he was sure of it — laughter, her laughter. He moved into the woods a little further, following a path dimly lit by the moon. He paused to listen, head tilted to the side. It was there, louder this time. He had to get away. He began to trot along the path, watching his footing amidst the leaves and the roots, until finally he was running. The laughter was everywhere now, surrounding him. He couldn't get away from it. He was running wildly now, stumbling over roots and rocks, gasping for breath, his head a crown of pain.

Roger never saw the drop. He simply ran off the side of a steep hill, rolling and tumbling to come to rest in the jumbled boulders at the bottom, his head twisted grotesquely to one side.

—•••••—

Mrs. Bratton found the telegram from Joe Spencer inside the mail slot. The woman from the telegraph office tried to deliver it to the hotel and Tackett told her where to find Roger Nolen. Joe Spencer thought Roger should know they found Martha's body beneath some underbrush about a mile downstream from the wrecked car.

The search for Roger Nolen was perfunctory, especially since no one pressed it. Some hunters happened upon his remains a year or so later, but no one could imagine how he came to be there.

The Searchers

I'd never known anybody really named Luke, that is until I moved here to the farm and met Luke Strange. A fittin' name for the man, I might add, since strange he was in a lot of ways. I'm a widower, and since I retired from the railroad I live up here in the hills of West Virginia. I rent this here old farmhouse, and Luke Strange lives in the next hollow. He's my closest neighbor, and we seem to favor each other's company. We walk together right much and from time to time share a meal, just for the company. I expect we get on so well because neither of us talk too much. We can walk the country roads together or sit and whittle for hours without swappin' more'n a dozen words. But I expect it's just comfortable being with other folks once in a while.

It wouldn't be hard to describe Luke physically. He was a big man, tall and raw-boned with thinning white hair and a combed beard. Wore bib overalls and flannel shirts mostly and rough work shoes. Old men who live alone tend to let themselves go; it's hard when you got nobody to look nice for. But not Luke. He was almost always scrubbed and shiny, and his clothes was clean and mended. Made me think a bit and begin to take more pains with my own bathin' and shavin' and laundry.

Describin' Luke as a person is something else again. We'd walk over the hills together, and he was forever scannin' the sky about us. As we'd come up each rise he'd stand and search the hills and horizon in every direction. I asked him once what he was lookin' for, but he just smiled a little and shook his head. He was good company though, and I felt a funny kind of peace and contentment when I was with him.

From time to time I would get to feelin' a little sad and alone and I'd drink a mite too much. How Luke knew about this I'll never know, but he'd always turn up at my place and sit with me until I sobered up or slept it off. I'd feel guilty about his seein' me this way, and I got to drinkin' less and less as a result.

Once in our travels, Luke cut off a country road near his place onto a little used path into the woods. It was carefully hidden from the road and only somebody familiar with the path could've found it. The path wound around through the woods, switchin' back from time to time so's you could see the way you'd come, always climbin' higher and higher into the hills. Finally it wound its way through a cleft in the rocks no wider'n a doorway, and we were in a hollow completely covered by an umbrella of trees. There, nestled against the hillside, was an old still — a large mash pot with a copper cover and a coil that must've been a hundred years old. All this was in a jumbled heap alongside a firebox made out'a stone with a short, wide chimney. There was the remains of a stack of cord wood that looked rotten and crumbly, with toadstools growin' here and there. No one'd used this here still for a long time.

In spite of this, I was nervous and eager to get away. Folks hereabouts don't take kindly to strangers pokin' around in their private places. This was akin to peekin' at their women folks bathin' in the creek. I began to wave at Luke, afraid to call out or even whisper, but he just shook his head and beckoned me to come sit aside him on a log. He told me this was his still and had been his daddy's and grand-daddy's before him. He took up a stick to whittle and began to tell me this story, which you ain't likely to believe, cause I found it hard believin' it myself.

Seems old Luke had been a heller in his younger days. He was a farmer by day and a moonshiner by night. Now that ain't too out of the ordinary in these parts, and the law don't bother you much if you just run enough for yourself and your family — maybe a friend or two. They don't look kindly 'tall if you run it up into jugs and sell it over to Giles County or down into Carolina. Uncle Sam wants his share, you know. Well, anyways, Luke had a reputation for runnin' clean stuff. You wasn't likely to go blind drinkin' his white lightnin'. After the war everybody and his brother tried runnin' corn, and they used old truck radiators and what-all for their mix. For a while they had more folks dyin' of lead poisonin' around these parts without a gun ever bein' fired. Old Luke had a '56 Buick that somebody'd done magic to. It could outrun anythin' this side of Roanoke, and he knew the mountain roads like a mama knows the face of her child.

From what he told me, he was a womanizer and a brawler too, just to make life interestin'. Half the treasury men east of the Mississippi knew about old Luke in one way or another. Local law men and their deputies used to dream about catchin' old Luke the way some folks dream about hittin' the lottery. He got chased after and shot at a few times, and he shot back a few times cause that's the way the game was played, but nobody could prove nothin' on him. Once he was followed right close by a deputy from over in Tennessee who had a hopped-up Pontiac. But he didn't know the roads like Luke, and when he come roarin' up a set of hairpin turns, Luke was waitin' on the next level and shot out his front tire. The car went skiddin' over the edge and got wedged between two trees about a hundred feet down the slope. Luke worked his way down the hill on foot and pulled the guy outta the wreck and made sure somebody knew where to come get him.

They finally got a task force together, some treasury agents from Charlestown and Morgantown, some ABC fellers from the capital and some mean-ass sheriff from over Parkersburg way who would've arrested his own daddy for spittin' on the sidewalk. They snooped and planned and finally ambushed old Luke one rainy night just the other side of the Twin Forks bridge. They was more interested in killin' him than catchin' him, cause they shot up his car right smart. In the whippin' rain and confusion Luke got away from the car and into the woods. They was sure they hit him at least once, maybe twice. Wasn't no use tryin' to track him in the dark and rain, so they waited there and sent for some bloodhounds. But the rain washed away the scent, tracks and bloodstains, and they had nothin'.

Luke worked his way over the mountain and up through the rocks to a lean-to in the hollow near his still. Then he passed out. He woke up about dawn, cold and wet, shiverin' and weak as a half-drowned kitten. He felt inside his coat and his shirt was crusted with blood. His side was burnin' and throbbin' with pain. He looked outside through the leafless trees and could see somethin' hoverin' over the cleft of rocks that surrounded the hollow. At first he thought it was a chopper searchin' out his hidin' place, but there was no throbbin' beat of the chopper blades, only a soft hissin' sound like air escapin' from an air jet. From the looks of it, at least what he could see of it, the thing was too big to be a chopper anyways. He just laid there in the lean-to and watched the dark shape move slightly from one side to the other and come lower and lower until it darkened the sky over the ravine.

Luke decided he was goin' to die, just a little sooner than he expected, and he accepted it. He'd been told a year or so earlier by some doctor down in Beckley that he had cirrhosis of the liver and if he kept drinkin' his own corn it'd kill him. By his own reckonin' Luke allowed as how he was his own best whiskey customer, but he didn't quit drinkin'. Now he lay sprawled there, bleedin' and light headed, and watched more with curiosity than fear as this big thing came closer and closer, and then he slipped off into a coma.

———•••●••———

He woke up in a funny lookin' room that was shaped like the inside of a bubble. At first he figured he was in some new, modern Federal jail since the walls looked like metal, maybe stainless steel. He was lyin' on what he thought was a cot or a bunk, but when he raised his head to look there was nothin' beneath him. That startled him some. It was like he was restin' on a cushion of air that just seemed to support him and wrap itself all around him. He was bucknaked, but whatever was wrapped around him and holdin' him up was warm and soothin'. He looked down at his side and there were three small, red pucker marks, all healed over. He tried to reach out and touch them, but he was unable to move his arms or hands more than a few inches. In fact he couldn't move his legs either.

Luke wanted to know what was happenin', and he tried to call out, but not a sound came from his mouth. He began to think he was drugged, and that made him scared. He began to look around the bubble. The inside seemed solid, with no openings or even seams to show where windows or doors might be. There were no lights, yet the inside of the bubble glowed like the dash lights on some fancy cars. He wondered how long he'd been there or how he came to be there. He was neither hungry nor thirsty, and he didn't have any pain, just a feelin' of warmth like sittin' in front of a cracklin' fire on a rainy night. What was even stranger was he had no cravin' for whiskey, none at all. In the past few years he had an almost continuous cravin' and could never go very long without whiskey. It'd gotten so he needed some first thing in the mornin' to start off his day. Now he was stretched out here, and he didn't seem to care if he ever tasted whiskey again and that puzzled him some.

Suddenly he was aware of a flickerin' area of light like foxfire on a rotten log. It got brighter and bigger until it was as big as those balloons they sell at the County fair, maybe three feet across. It moved toward him and came to a floatin' stop right alongside him. For some reason he wasn't scared, just curious, his mind full of questions. Then he was aware the ball of light was talkin' to him. Well, not talkin' like we're talkin' but communicatin' through his mind. It was tellin' him he was safe and healed and had nothin' to fear. Then, Luke thought, where am I? How did I get here? The answers came back as thoughts. He was found by chance, severely injured. He was with… the searchers… and he was being served.

Luke became aware of two other balls of light that had appeared in the bubble, but they were just there, not communicatin' with him. His mind began to race with questions. Who were the searchers? What were they searchin' for? Where did they come from? What did they want? Why did they pick him?

Then his thoughts stopped, almost as if somethin' put them on hold. Very slowly and carefully the answers began to come into his mind. The searchers are a peaceful life form from… far away. They are interested in life forms of this galaxy and are on a search mission. The words scientific and experimental streaked across his mind like flashes of lightnin' but were quickly gone. The thought came that further attempts to provide answers would be beyond his ability to understand. They would return him to where they found him. Will you ever come back, he thought, and immediately the answer came back: yes, of course. We find much merit in your species if directed to positive pursuits. We plan to try sometime in the future. The mind communicatin' was tiring, and Luke was suddenly exhausted. He drifted off into a deep, dreamless sleep.

Luke awoke to the sound of wind in the trees, layin' in the lean-to, the autumn sun reflectin' off the rock walls of the ravine and warmin' the area. He was dressed as he was the night of the ambush except his clothes were clean, dry and without bullet holes or bloodstains. He pulled his coat and shirt open to reveal three puckered bullet scars healed over with healthy new skin. There wasn't any stiffness nor pain when he moved. And even more startlin', the skin of his body was pink and healthy without the muddy, yellowish look he had come to know as a result of the cirrhosis. He never felt so good, so healthy, so content. He'd gotten to his feet, walked to the still and proceeded to push and kick it into the scattered heap that now lay before him.

Now, I don't really think of myself as an educated man, though I almost finished the eleventh grade before I quit to go to work on the railroad. In spite of my limits I reckon I had to do a little detective work, if only to set my own mind to rest. The next time I took the old pick-up down to Streitville for supplies, I found myself drivin' right on through and on to Beckley. Used the yellow pages and a pay phone outside Hardee's to call. On the fourth try I talked with the Doctor who'd seen Luke. I let on like I was Luke's uncle from Tennessee and needed to know how bad off old Luke was. He surely left no doubt in my mind that Luke Strange was dyin' of the cirrhosis. He was a mite surprised old Luke was still livin'.

I thought 'bout that all the way back to Streitville. I stopped at Erna's Cafe to have a beer and a hamburger, but more to talk to old Pap Sanders. I bought him two cans of Bud, and he was more than happy to tell me about Luke Strange and the night he bought the farm at the Twin Forks bridge. Pap says he counted thirty-seven bullet holes in Luke's old Buick when they towed her in, enough blood on the floor and seat to open a blood bank. There wasn't no way he could've lived too long after that. It didn't make no difference to Pap that the fella up to the farm said he was Luke. All the folks hereabouts knows it's his brother Virgil up there to the farm. Why, even the sheriff and the Treasury dudes know it ain't Luke, or they'd a gone up after him afore now. Besides, that dude up there is too healthy to be Luke. Everybody knows if he hadn't been shot he'd a been dead long ago from the booze.

— • • ● ● • —

Nowadays when Luke and me go walkin' the back roads I find myself pausin' on the rises and carefully searchin' the hills and horizon in all directions right along with Luke. After all, he did show me three pucker scars that day up to the still site. And who knows, maybe his story is true. I can tell you one thing for sure, I ain't never seen a healthier, more contented man in my whole life.

Rachel's Run

Rachel Porter set the grocery bag down on a chair and bumped the door with her hip to close it. She flipped through the mail to find three bills and two pieces of junk mail addressed to resident. She kicked off her shoes, turned on the TV and sank into an armchair. The news about the fire in Edgeton held her attention even though she wasn't particularly interested. It took her mind off the dullness of the day at the shop. Most days she could take in all the small talk and gossip without letting it bother her. Often she joined right in, but today it all seemed to close in on her until she felt trapped. That's been happening a lot lately, she thought. The phone rang, and she got up to answer it, thinking it would probably be someone trying to sell her something. This time of day was their favorite time to call.

"Hello!"

"Hello." It was a man's voice, and there was a pause.

"Hello," she said again.

"If you didn't want to go out to dinner with me, all you had to do was say no."

Rachel paused, her brows knit together in a puzzled expression. "Who is this anyway?"

"Well, how many dinner invitations have you passed up lately?"

There was silence, and Rachel, suddenly alert, asked, "Is this Rob Tucker?"

"Yeah, it's me. And I guess that means I must've been the only one you refused to have dinner with."

"Where are you, Rob? Where are you calling from?" Rachel was pleased and a little excited. It had to be a month, no, more than two months since she had met Rob Tucker in Bramwell.

"I'm right here in Kelsoe, at a place called the Crossroads Diner. I was wondering if I could get a straight answer from you tonight about joining me for dinner?"

"What are you doing in Kelsoe?"

"At the moment trying to get you to go to dinner, or at least getting to hear you say no outright."

She laughed at that, remembering the last time he had called and asked her. "I'm sorry. I guess I deserved that."

"Uh-huh!"

"Well, you don't need to rub it in, you know." He didn't answer.

"Yes, Rob, I'll meet you for dinner, but not at the Crossroads Diner."

Well, this isn't the kind of place I had in mind either. Since this is your town, I'll ask you to pick out someplace nice."

"OK! Why don't you just stay there, and I'll come meet you in about an hour."

"Fair enough. I'll be here."

Rachel stood leaning against the wall by the kitchen phone and thought about that day in Bramwell. She'd driven there to bury her father and was remembering some of the unhappy times there. When the police cruiser pulled up behind her, she was sure she was going to get a traffic ticket, but it turned out differently. The man in uniform, Rob Tucker, turned out to be kind and helpful. She couldn't believe how excited she felt about seeing him again. After the funeral he'd called and asked her out to dinner. She had been evasive and promised to call him back, but she never did. Instead she'd simply left town. She kept warning herself that it was probably some big joke. He was really going to get even for her standing him up that last day in Bramwell. Rachel was afraid to admit to herself how often she had thought about him these past months, and how often she'd wished she had accepted his invitation. Now here he was in Kelsoe, for whatever reason, and had found her. It couldn't be real; it had to be some kind of sick joke. But, she thought, I'll just have to take that chance.

———•••••———

"Finding you was easy. Getting to know you is another matter altogether. Now I'm not so sure it was a good idea." He paused, thinking out his words, finally shaking his head, "I guess I wasn't expecting it to be so complicated."

Rachel sat across from him silent and attentive. Her expression was serious and offered nothing, neither approval nor rejection. He waited for some sign from her, some reaction to what he had said, but there was none.

"We didn't see that much of each other, just a couple of chance meetings, no more than a few hours all told, and yet..." He paused again, shaking his head.

"Why did you feel you had to find me?" Her voice was soft with a note of urgency, almost a demand for rationality.

"I don't know. I really don't. Let's just say there was something about you that made me want to see you again. I guess that sounds a little odd, doesn't it? When I called that day after your father's funeral you could have ended it. Why didn't you?"

It was her turn to pause and shake her head, "I don't know either. I guess I was running again."

He looked puzzled. "From me?"

"No, Rob, not from you. From everything: the town, the past, from all the memories that have haunted me through the years," she stopped and then added, "from myself. Maybe I should have been more honest with you when you called. I'm sorry."

"It's OK. It's just that I kept wondering why you did that. I thought asking you to dinner after the funeral might have offended you."

She shook her head and looked down into the wine glass as she twirled the stem gently. "No, it wasn't that at all. The truth is I wanted to see you again that night, but I was afraid."

"Afraid of what?"

"I guess I was afraid," she stopped and looked up at him, "of how it would turn out."

Rob looked puzzled, but he didn't say anything. Rachel turned away, staring out the window into the darkness, barely able to see the outline of the trees across the pond. The waitress came by and poured more coffee for them and left.

"I'm not sure I can make you understand, Rob. Bramwell was a part of my life that was nothing but bitterness and trouble. I couldn't get away from there fast enough. And when I did leave it was under a cloud. Going back, even for a little while, brought it all crowding back in on me. Sounds ridiculous, doesn't it?"

"Not if that's what you feel. Look, whatever your reasons were for leaving, they're not important, at least not to me. So long as it wasn't me you were running from. I'd like to see you again, Rachel. Would that be all right?"

"Why, Rob?"

"I said it earlier. There's something about you that makes me want to see you again. I enjoyed tonight, the dinner, your company. Do I need more of a reason?"

"You're going to drive two hundred miles to see me and maybe take me out to dinner? Really?"

"Yeah, well, it's only a hundred-eighty-two miles. I found a short cut. Besides, I might need to get away from Bramwell once in a while, too, you know." He was smiling now, "Can I call you when I come again?"

Rachel nodded slowly. She found herself drifting into the wariness she always felt nagging at her when she couldn't guess at people's motives, but she shunted it aside. Rachel wanted to believe he was coming all that way just to see her. It made her feel warm, wanted, important. She reveled in it, knowing in the back of her mind it might turn out to be nothing, a counterfeit, a failure like so many relationships had been before.

"You said my reasons for leaving Bramwell weren't important to you. How can you be so sure? You don't know anything about me." There was a note of earnestness in her voice.

"Well, you don't know much about me either, so we're even. We'll have time to learn about each other, I hope."

And they left it at that. He followed her home in his car.

— • • ● • • —

Rachel sat in the dark staring out the window through the filmy curtains watching the changing patterns of light as the breeze ruffled the trees. It's crazy to begin to get involved with him, she kept telling herself. It couldn't work, ever. His job's in Bramwell. He's been there for years. I'd never go back, even if it got serious enough for him to ask me. Now that Papa's dead, the last link is broken. I can't bear to think of beginning a new one. Why can't I ever get away from that damned town?

Rob had followed her to her apartment. He had come in for a few minutes, but made no effort to stay. He'd asked once more if he could see her again and she agreed. As he was opening the door he leaned back and kissed her on the cheek, and then he was gone. She felt guilty about her suspicions when he'd asked if he could come in. But then, she thought, old habits are hard to break.

Rachel dreamt about her father that night, a distorted, fragmentary account of Bramwell and all the old troubles. She wakened with a start and got up to wander around the apartment in the half light. It was almost six, the first faint tint of dawn brightening the sky and filtering into the room where she sat. She wanted a cigarette badly. The craving was there even though she hadn't smoked since that last visit to Bramwell. Rachel was annoyed and wondered why her life suddenly seemed so disjointed.

Thinking back on it, she guessed she knew about Papa and Mildred long before she was old enough to realize it. Even when she was ten or eleven, she was aware her older sister was afraid of him, just the way Mama was. He had a way of looking that would stop Mama, and Mildred, too, in mid-sentence, and they'd turn away and go quietly about their business.

Not her, though. She'd argue with him, and ask why when she wasn't supposed to, and get smacked some for it. But it didn't stop her. Mama and Mildred would look scared when she challenged Papa, like they expected something bad to happen. But most of the time he'd act like he enjoyed her spunk, standing up to him that way. There were also times when he didn't think it was cute and she was punished, grounded, and even tanned now and then. Papa was a great one for using his belt.

Rachel thought back to that rainy night it all changed from vague suspicion to hard reality. The thunder had wakened her, and she heard the first scattering of rain on the porch roof outside her window. The curtains began to blow, and, only half awake, she went to close the window. There, standing by the open window, she heard Mildred crying softly. The window to Mildred's room was the next one down. Then she heard her father's muffled voice telling Mildred to be quiet. Rachel never spoke about that to anyone — not Mildred, not Mama, not anyone. But suddenly everything was so painfully clear. She kept wondering if anyone else knew — the neighbors, people at school, but most of all, Mama.

After that night her life changed. She began to run with Sylvia Sturn and that crowd. She started smoking and got suspended from school. A little later she began drinking and was brought home by a deputy. Papa used his belt that night, and she was grounded indefinitely, but she didn't care. The big problems came after she was caught smoking pot. Mama cried, and Papa raged. He restricted her every move for a while. Rachel learned to bend and finally break every rule he set, and she was sure he knew some of it was happening. But by now her reputation around town as a wild one was well established.

One afternoon, about a year later, Mildred came home early from her job at the bank. She told them at work she was sick, but she wasn't. Mildred hurriedly packed her belongings and left Bramwell on a Trailways bus, and Mama made no move to stop her. While she was packing, Mildred told Rachel to watch out for Papa, especially when he's acting like he's drunk. Rachel remembered the scene Papa made, screaming at Mama for not stopping Mildred from leaving, and Mama never answered him. He tried to find out where she went, but her ticket was to a transfer terminal in Emoryville, and she could have gone almost anywhere from there. Rachel could remember her feelings then, a sense of sadness and loss, and apprehension. Nothing seemed to matter anymore. It was as if she was waiting for something to happen; she wasn't sure what.

And then came the night that was to become the ongoing nightmare she'd lived with and dreamt about again and again over the years, and once the events began to unfold in her mind she couldn't stop them. It was like running down a steep hill, going faster and faster, unable to stop.

Rachel got up from the chair and switched on the TV. She needed to clear her mind of all the old, bitter memories. Lord knows she'd been over and through them more times than she cared to remember. She walked to the kitchen, started a pot of coffee, and came back to stand in the doorway trying to concentrate on the morning news, but she couldn't. Finally she switched off the set and walked to the window. She was ready to accept the fact that she could not put an end to the chronology of past events she'd been reliving in her mind.

He swore later he was only trying to pull the covers up over her. The night had turned cold, and he'd come to shut the window and be sure she was properly covered, or so he said. It wasn't something he usually did, but she could never convince anyone of that. She was awakened by his fumbling with the covers, and when she gasped he put his hand over her mouth and told her to be quiet. She could remember trying to push him away, but he held her down. She was frightened and began to thrash about, and her hand fell on the scissors on the night table alongside the bed.

She never could remember the details of what happened after that. It was all a jumble of shouts and curses, her own screams, and Mama frozen in the doorway, her hand still on the light switch. Papa lay sprawled on the floor alongside her bed, his hands clutching his leg above the scissors embedded in his thigh.

The reaction throughout Bramwell was shock, followed by disbelief and then anger. She remembered Chief Titus' statement about her possession and use of marijuana and the principal's report of the drinking incidents at school, as well as other discipline problems and subsequent suspensions. And so it went. The parade of incidents, none of them significant in themselves, but taken together created a portrait of defiant incorrigibility for the juvenile judge.

Her accusations only seemed to be a desperate attempt to justify what had happened. The fact that the judge and Chief Titus were part of Papa's poker and drinking crowd didn't help much. Papa lied, Mama remained silent, and Mildred was nowhere to be found.

The two years she spent at the women's reformatory in Ravenswood were like the dim, recurring memories of an old horror movie. Isolated incidents tumbled through her mind as sharp and vivid as the day she lived them. The rest was a hazy, nebulous jumble of sights, and sounds, and smells rolling through her subconscious like a videotape on fast forward. It was at Ravenswood she learned the rudiments of her trade as a beautician. That was the only plus in the whole experience.

Mama died while she was at Ravenswood; she refused the furlough they offered her to attend the funeral. Rachel was released when she was eighteen and never went home again. And too many things, good and bad, had happened in the years between.

Rachel left the window and walked across the room to sit at the desk. She sat staring at the phone. Finally she took out some note paper and began to write.

Rob,

I think it would be better for us both if we didn't see each other again. Please accept my decision and don't ask for an explanation because I'm not sure I can give one. This really has nothing to do with you, or who you are. Believe me when I say this is really for the best.

Rachel Porter

Rachel never opened the two letters he sent, and she bought an answering machine to screen her calls. The letters stopped, and in a few weeks the calls ended, too. Some things Rob said on that last recorded call stayed with her long after all else was forgotten. He said she couldn't run forever, especially from herself. He also said they could have made it together, and there was a note of sadness in his voice that haunted her. Rachel played that message over and over again before she finally erased it.

It was hard to remember what happened those three weeks after that last recorded call. Rachel went to the shop each day and did her work, but she was never really with it. Her thoughts were a kaleidoscope of images and impressions of the few brief encounters in Bramwell and the night they had dinner together. Then one afternoon she decided she could not put him behind her as she had done with so many others in the past. She left the shop and went home to place a person-to-person call to Rob at the Police Station in Bramwell. The dispatcher informed her that Officer Tucker was no longer employed there. Rachel replaced the phone in the cradle and sat staring at it as if it had betrayed her. Then she put her head down on her arms and wept for the first time in years.

———•••••——

As winter settled in, Rachel seized upon a project she had only half considered in the past, a new beauty shop in Hermitage. The shop in Kelsoe was well established with a steady, loyal clientele. Hermitage had just the one shop called The Beauty Bar run by Verna Epperson and her sister, Edna Inge. Both ladies were widows and getting on in years, and while the older women were comfortable with their services, most of the younger set came to one of the shops in Kelsoe. Those who commuted to Edgeton usually went to one of the half dozen or so shops there or stopped in Kelsoe on their way back to Hermitage.

Rumor had it that Verna and Edna were thinking about retiring and moving to Florida. To be honest, Rachel had been hearing that from various sources for over a year. Maybe, she thought, they just needed someone to make them an offer. It was worth a try. On a Tuesday morning in November, Rachel drove to Hermitage and arrived just as the sisters were opening up for the day. She followed them into the shop as they unlocked the door. Two hours later they had reached an agreement.

That was the beginning of what was to become a mad scramble for a bank loan, a lawyer, a contractor and meetings with Shana Rucker about managing the new location. The goal of having the shop ready by mid-December meant countless trips and meetings to iron out the details. Rachel began to feel like a commuter between Kelsoe and Hermitage.

Late one afternoon, after a meeting with the contractor in Hermitage, Rachel started back to Kelsoe. The weather was cold and the rain was turning to sleet as she drove out of town. A few miles out of town it turned into a heavy, wet snow. The worst part of the trip was just ahead, six or seven miles of curving roads through a hilly area. She debated with herself about turning back to spend the night at a motel in Hermitage. She decided to try and make it home. Riding slowly down a curving turn to the left her car began to slip and slide to the right. It was over in a matter of seconds, almost before she realized she was in trouble. The low speed allowed the car to slide off the road and come to rest with the rear wheels in a shallow ditch. The spinning wheels as she tried to get out only succeeded in digging her in deeper until finally she stopped trying.

Traffic had been light, but someone must have reported her car off the road because within twenty minutes or so a State Police cruiser pulled onto the shoulder just past her car. The trooper sat talking on his radio for a minute or so before coming back to speak with her. The broad brim on his hat and the turned up collar of his coat masked his face as he worked his way down to her car. Rachel only half watched his approach as she fumbled in her purse for her license and registration, thinking she would need to show them. And then he was standing alongside her car. She rolled down the mist-coated window and there stood Rob Tucker.

The shock of recognition left them both speechless for a few moments. Rob was the first to recover.

"Rachel! Are you all right? Do you need an ambulance?"

Rachel sat there, totally confused, mouth open in surprise.

He asked again, "Are you hurt, Rachel? Shall I call for help?"

She shook her head. "I'm all right, I think. I'm just so cold." She paused, "But what are you doing here? How did you get here? Oh, Rob, I'm so glad to see you."

———•••••———

Rachel sat in the police cruiser, engine idling, the heater on high. At least she was warm but still so confused. How is it he's here, she kept asking herself.

Rob was talking to the driver of the tow truck, giving him directions about where to take the car. Finally he came back to the cruiser and sat making notes in his log book. He looked over at her and smiled as he continued writing for a few more minutes. He closed the log and turned to her.

"I have instructions to take you home. Your vehicle may have been damaged and be unsafe to drive. Do you want to go home or should I drop you somewhere else?"

"No, Rob, that's fine. I'd like to go home."

He pulled the cruiser onto the road and started toward Kelsoe. He radioed his time and destination. It was getting dark now but the snow had tapered off somewhat. They rode in silence for a while until Rachel could no longer hold her curiosity. She asked the same questions she had asked earlier, "What are you doing here? How did you get here?"

Rob shook his head slowly as he began to speak, "That night I called you from the Crossroads Diner?" She nodded and he continued, "I'd spent the whole day at the Police Barracks in Edgeton taking tests and a physical for the State Police."

"Why didn't you tell me that night?"

"I didn't know if I'd be accepted. There didn't seem to be much point in talking about something that might not happen. There would have been enough time to talk about it when I saw you again. Only I never did see you again."

"Why did you leave Bramwell? You must have had some years of seniority. Why?"

"I guess I knew three or four years ago that the job in Bramwell was a dead end. A comfortable dead end, but a dead end nonetheless. Maybe meeting you touched something in me to get me moving." He grinned, "Maybe you made me suddenly aware of another world outside of Bramwell."

"Rob, do you know anything about me and my family?"

"Yeah, I know about your father and your reputation for being a wild one. I also know about Ravenswood and how you came to be there."

Rachel had her head down so he couldn't see her face in the reflected light from the dashboard.

"I think you should know, Rachel, that I knew all that before I called you that night from the Crossroads Diner. I told you then it didn't matter and I'll say it again. It's not who you were then, it's who you are now that matters." He waited for her to respond, but she was silent, so he continued, "You never read my letters or you'd know all this. You wouldn't answer my calls, and I got tired of talking to your damned machine."

They were in Kelsoe now, only a few blocks from her home. Rachel needed to say something, but she wasn't sure where to begin. Rob pulled in front of her house and waited, leaning forward, forearms draped over the steering wheel.

"Rachel, the last thing I said to you on the machine was that I thought we could make it if we gave it half a chance. I still feel that way." He hesitated and added, "But I want you to know I'm not going to bother you. If you don't want to see me again tell me to my face, right now, and I'll be on my way."

Rachel turned to face him, her eyes bright with tears. She sat looking at him in silence and then answered softly, "Yes, Rob, I do want to see you again. I'd like to get to know you, really know you. As it is you know so much about me and my life and I know so little about you. If," she hesitated, unsure of how he would take what she wanted to say, "you care to see me on those terms, at least until I — we are more comfortable with each other, then I want to see you."

Rob showed no reaction. His expression was serious as he listened carefully to what she had to say.

She continued, "You were right when you said I couldn't keep running forever, but it's hard to stop, to learn to trust again. Can you understand what I'm trying to say?" There was no mistaking the earnestness in her voice.

His serious expression opened into an easy smile and he nodded. "I understand, Rachel. I'm glad you've decided to give us a chance to make it work. Go on in now and get warm, have something hot to drink. I'll call you tomorrow, and I'll see you soon."

Something of Consequence

*L*inda Parelli handed her husband a mug of hot soup and plopped down beside him on the couch, one leg curled beneath her. She watched silently as he spooned up the soup.

"It's almost eleven. Do you want to watch the news?" she asked.

"Not tonight. Let's just talk a while. We never seem to get a chance to talk very often. Are the kids all right? Is Kevin's cold any better?"

"He still has the sniffles, but he hasn't had a fever since yesterday. I think he'll probably go to school tomorrow. The baby is great. She's eating us out of house and home, and she's doing the cutest things. I wouldn't let her play with Kevin because of his cold, so she was hiding behind the door to his room playing peek-a-boo with him this morning. He got a big kick out of that."

There was silence as each seemed caught up in his own thoughts. Finally Linda broke the silence with a question, "What is it, Drew? Did something happen today?"

He took a deep breath and stretched his arms out before him, moving his shoulders from side to side. "Two or three things, I hardly know where to start. The wicked witch was in to observe me this morning. That makes three times in the last two weeks. I had a visit from Mrs. Seitz, the psychologist, and I got a new kid in class this afternoon. That makes thirty-one. Which reminds me, I have a spelling test to mark for tomorrow."

"What did she want? Mrs. Seitz, I mean."

"She took up almost my whole lunch period telling me about this new girl who was coming into my class. Her name is Kristal Scruggs, and it seems she was taken out of the home because of child abuse. Her mother's live-in boy friend was sexually abusing her. You know Seitz, I got a big buildup about what a good teacher I am and how they gave it a lot of thought before they decided to assign her to my class. I felt like saying, 'Don't clap, throw money,' but I didn't. She'd probably take it back to the wicked witch."

"What's she like, the new girl?"

"She's a skinny little thing with stringy hair and bruises on her legs. She doesn't look like she's ever had a decent meal, or any love either. She's silent. She doesn't speak if she can get by with a nod. When she does speak it's almost a whisper. She looks like a frightened animal ready to run."

"The poor thing. She's probably had a miserable time of it. Why do people do things like that, I wonder? What do you suppose is on Ms. Beech's mind?"

"I wish I knew. It's too early in the school year for her to be thinking about next year's contracts. It's only October. Maybe there's been a complaint about me from one of the parents, but I'm damned if I can figure out why, or who." He paused and added, "She knows I'm working outside of school, but then so are a lot of the others. Maybe she's trying to see if I'm preparing for my classes properly. You never know with her until the ax falls."

"You're always prepared, aren't you, Drew?"

"Of course I am. You know better than that, Linda."

"I've been giving a whole lot of thought to Bill Knight's proposition. Maybe he's right; maybe it is time for me to think about getting out of teaching. There sure doesn't seem to be any chance to go anywhere in this system. It's so damned big they hardly even know I exist, except for Beech's poop list." They lapsed into silence, mulling over what had just been said. Drew continued, "You know, Linda, the kids are getting big, and I feel like I'm missing out on the best part of it. And besides that, we never seem to get ahead, financially. We could probably take the money we're saving for a house and blow it all on one good dinner and a movie."

"Come on, Drew, that's an exaggeration and you know it. The question you have to come to grips with is do you want to be in the real estate management business? Are you going to be happy with that for life? Of course there's the bigger question, which I'm sure hasn't escaped you: namely, where do we get the money for our share in the business? I know you don't want to just work for him."

"Yeah! Managing property while he sells real estate and makes big commissions is one thing, but forever, I just don't know. I do know that he's making one helluva lot more money than he ever did teaching, and there's something to be said for that."

"Oh Drew, we've been over this so many times, it's like being on a merry-go-round. It's late, and we're both tired. No more tonight. We aren't going to come to any earth-shattering decisions tonight."

They walked down the hall to the bedroom with their arms around each other, and he thought how lucky he was to have her. He stopped to peek in at the kids and marveled at the angelic look about them as they slept.

———•••••—

There were seven fourth-grade sections at Mark Wood Elementary School, and Andrew Parelli was the only male teacher at that grade level. It was logical, he thought, that Kristal Scruggs had been placed in his class; she needed to learn to interact with men again. It would be difficult for her, he knew. She was going to have a hard time learning to trust again.

He'd been shaken that morning by her reaction when he'd leaned over to point out an error in the arithmetic exercise she was working on. She had winced, cringed really, as he reached past her to show her the mistake. She expected to be struck. Her arm came up to shield her face as she ducked away from him, and then she was embarrassed. Drew acted as if none of it had happened as he drew her attention to the error in subtraction. He spoke softly and smiled at her as he moved on up the aisle to check the work of others.

Kristal Scruggs had been startled. Drew Parelli had noticed how she kept careful track of his whereabouts in the classroom. During regular class activities this was not difficult. It was only when they were assigned reading or other desk work that Kristal constantly checked to see where he was. Today she had evidently become engrossed in her work and let her guard down.

At lunch time teachers led their classes to the huge cafeteria and sat with the children while they ate their lunch. It was a cheap and easy way to maintain control. Most of the children brown-bagged it, very few bought lunch, and never on a regular basis. They were allowed to play outdoors after they'd eaten, so most of them wolfed down their food and left for the playground. Then Drew would take his own lunch up to the teacher's lounge and try to relax for a half hour before the resumption of classes.

He began to think about the after-school job. Usually he marked papers or gave extra help until four, then it was off to make the rounds of the small apartment buildings Bill Knight managed under contract. Drew collected rents, verified the need for repairs as reported by the tenants and contacted the repair service that handled that end of things.

Drew was only half aware of the small talk and banter from the other teachers who shared the first lunch period. Indeed, he hardly ever saw any of the other faculty who worked in the building. He finished lunch and started back to his classroom, determined to finish grading yesterday's spelling test. Ms. Beech was waiting for him.

"Good afternoon, Mr. Parelli. Have you finished lunch?"

"Yes, and I came back early to finish grading a spelling test. Is there something you need from me?"

"No. I plan to observe and just arrived a little early." She smiled.

Ms. Beech was trim, well-groomed and very businesslike. Rumor had it that she was married at one time, but no one knew for sure whether she was widowed or divorced. She had a well-deserved reputation for being aloof, demanding and uncompromising. Every year there were at least three or four teachers who left, either by transfer or by non-renewal of contract.

Ms. Beech observed everyone. She would walk into a room unannounced and fully expect that teacher not to miss a beat in the lesson being taught. She might stay for ten minutes or all morning, and this practice applied to all staff, veterans who had been there longer than she had, as well as "Rookies." At Mark Wood, "Rookies" were teachers with less than three years experience.

Drew mentally wrestled with himself for a few moments and finally decided to confront her with his concerns. "Ms. Beech, is there some question about the quality of my teaching, or perhaps my lesson preparation?"

She turned from reading his notes on the blackboard and her head came up as she fixed him with a stare. "Observing and evaluating teachers is my job, Mr. Parelli. I do it when and with whomever I please. Do you have a problem with that?"

"No, of course not. It's just that..." he paused and she finished it for him.

"I seem to be overdoing it in your case?"

They stood staring at each other in silence as the children began to filter back into the room, laughing and talking until they saw Ms. Beech and then reverting to whispers.

Drew Parelli taught the best social studies lesson ever, he thought. And the kids were with him all the way. As he was writing the homework assignment on the board Ms. Beech rose from the desk at the back of the room and quietly left. In spite of himself, Drew felt a nagging sense of apprehension, almost as if she knew something he didn't which he had no way to defend against.

—••●●•—

The Airways District of Edgeton was a sprawling, working class, payday-to-payday kind of neighborhood bordering the far end of the airport, away from the city. It was made up of two-, three- and four-family houses with a scattering of small apartment buildings throughout. It wasn't too far from Mark Wood Elementary School, and many of the younger children attended there. Most of the smaller multi-family houses were owner-occupied. The apartment houses and many of the three- and four-family houses were owned by a real estate partnership. It was this group that contracted with Bill Knight for management services. Most of the tenants Drew collected from paid their rent in cash, and he wrote receipts. Very few had checking accounts. And since a vast majority were working parents, Drew made his rent rounds in the early evening. Often he was concerned about the cash he was forced to carry and would interrupt his rounds to make two, sometimes three, night deposits at the airport bank drop. Some rents were collected mid-month and some at the beginning. So, twice each month Drew would make the rounds, and it usually took a week to make all the collections. Late payers were a fact of life.

Each collection period he'd have to fill out some delinquency forms. He would try to make notations about layoffs, illnesses and the countless other minor catastrophes that bedeviled these people. Things like a car breakdown, a dead battery, a broken refrigerator, a sick child, doctor's bills and an expensive prescription could completely derail tight and fragile budgets. Drew hated that part of it, and more than once loaned money to some particularly strapped folks. Bill Knight called him a soft-hearted fool and predicted he'd never make it as a businessman. But Drew couldn't turn his back on them. He kept seeing himself and his own family.

It all came to a head just before Thanksgiving. Drew had been delayed by a particularly long and dreary faculty meeting and was more than an hour late meeting with Bill Knight. As he came into the small, storefront office, Bill was noticeably annoyed.

"You could have called, Drew. I've been sitting here on my dead ass waiting. I could've taken a client out to see some houses. Time is money in this damned business. You know that."

"Sure, I get up in the middle of a faculty meeting and tell Beech I've got to let my other employer know I'm gonna' be late. Be realistic, Bill, you were there once yourself."

"Yeah! Thank God that's over and done with. When are you going to make the jump into reality?"

"Look, let's not start that today. I've had a bitch of a day. Beech was in again today; that makes seven times, no eight, since early October."

"What's her problem?" Bill asked.

"Damned if I know. I asked her once if anything was wrong and she cut me off at the knees. I don't have a good feeling about this."

Bill looked interested as he listened. Usually he had little patience with Drew's school problems. "You sound worried. Are you?"

Drew really didn't want to discuss it. He was sure it would only lead to renewed pressure for him to leave teaching and come into the business. Finally he answered, "I suppose I am, a little. I can't seem to find a reason." He got up from his chair and walked to the front of the store to stare out into the lowering dusk. For once Bill didn't comment. Drew turned back, "If she peppered me with evaluation reports, I'd at least have some idea of what I was up against. But she hasn't sent any, not one." He came back to sit across the desk from Bill.

Bill rocked back in his chair and stretched before he leaned forward and began to speak, "I had a phone call today from Whetstein. They have an option to buy three eight-unit buildings over in the Little Warsaw section of town. He wanted to know if we'd manage them."

"What did you tell him?"

Knight rubbed his chin and sighed. "I told him I'd have to let him know. If the deal goes through it won't be until the end of January, or even into February next year. He didn't need a yes or no answer right away. We need to make some decisions, Drew."

Drew nodded but didn't say anything.

"Look, you put in between fifteen and twenty hours a week now and that's pretty nearly saturation for you. Don't get me wrong, Drew, you do a good job, but I need you full time if we are to grow." He waited for an answer.

It had been building to this point for the last few months, and Drew knew it. He had put the inevitable out of his mind so many times; now here it was demanding a decision he wasn't ready to make, not emotionally and certainly not financially. Deep down he knew he wanted to teach. He didn't have the money to buy into Bill Knight's business, and he'd never quit teaching just to work for him. That had always been his rationale, his logical reason for not leaving the profession. And he was ready to use it again.

"You know I don't have the money to buy in. And you also know I won't quit to become an employee. Nothing's changed, Bill."

"If you had the money to buy in, say ten thousand for a one-third interest, would you be interested?" Bill was staring at him. "Well, would you?"

There was a challenge in Bill's tone and Drew, suddenly alert, felt a sense of foreboding, a feeling that events were racing madly away and he had no control over them.

"You've been teaching seven, or is it eight years, Drew?"

"This is my eighth year," he answered.

"Well, you've been contributing to your pension fund, a fat chunk out of every pay check, these seven and a half years. That's your money, Drew, and it comes back to you with interest when you quit. I'll bet you have ten thousand, even a bit more." He smiled and pointed a finger. "It's decision time, Drew. Time to make some choices. Like they say, fish or cut bait."

———•••••———

"After all the discussion I told Bill we'd make a decision by the end of the year."

Linda felt Bill was pressuring Drew. "After all," she said, "The new apartment contract wasn't a done deal. It might never come to pass."

"If I only knew what was driving Ms. Beech. I hate to think she's trying to harass me into quitting or asking for a transfer."

Linda shook her head, mulling over all that had been discussed. Finally she said, "You realize that if you take your pension money you're closing the door, pretty much, on ever going back to teaching. You'd have to start over, or pay back what you withdrew."

That thought hung between them, ominous in its implications, a new facet to the already complicated tangle of events.

"We've got almost six weeks to decide, Linda. Let's just think it out and talk it out. We are going to decide this together. Whichever way we go it's going to affect the whole family."

She agreed as they began the nightly ritual of closing up the house and getting ready for bed. Both of them were busy with the avalanche of thoughts aroused by the discussion.

—•••••—

After that Drew went back to the classroom acutely aware of all the positive feelings he always had about teaching, and the negatives, too. Suddenly he was conscious of his own ability and the pleasure of watching as the children responded to his efforts. It was almost like being a new teacher all over again, only better.

The observations ceased as abruptly as they had begun and he rarely saw Ms. Beech, even in the corridors. The nagging shadow of misgiving, however, stayed with him, hovering just on the edge of things, and he was unable to will it away.

Kristal Scruggs began to come out of her sanctuaries a little more each day as the other children drew her into their activities. She had a nice, shy smile, Drew noticed, and answered readily when drawn into class discussions. He was pleasantly surprised when she came to his desk on her own for help with an arithmetic problem. She smiled and thanked him for the help. That was definitely one of the positives, he thought.

The days ran together in a jumble of rising excitement as Christmas drew near. The work outside school was hum-drum, and he saw little of Bill Knight. Nothing further was mentioned about coming into the business and for that he was grateful. The letter in his school mailbox on the Monday before Christmas was like retribution for the past carefree weeks in the classroom. The Superintendent of Schools imprint on the envelope was enough to make him wary. He thrust it in his briefcase unopened. Drew knew he needed to be alone when he read it. In his classroom he fumbled open the envelope to read:

Mr. Parelli:

Please report to my office on Tuesday, December 22nd at three-thirty PM. I have requested Ms. Beech to also attend this conference.

Arthur L. Peterson
Assistant Superintendent

———•••••—

Drew Parelli had given his name to the secretary and now sat waiting to be ushered into Dr. Peterson's office. Ms. Beech came into the office and nodded to Drew. The secretary waved her to go on in to Dr. Peterson's office, "Go right in, Ms. Beech. He's been waiting for you."

Drew glanced at his watch, 3:35. He wondered just how long he'd have to wait. He'd gone through every possible scenario as to why he'd been summoned and finally reasoned he was being terminated in midyear. But why? That left him with the same array of unanswered questions. It was only minutes before he was ushered inside. Dr. Peterson was cordial enough.

"Please, have a seat, Mr. Parelli." He was holding Drew's personnel folder as he asked, "May I call you Andrew?"

Before he could answer Ms. Beech interjected, "I believe he prefers to be called Drew. Am I right Mr. Parelli?"

"Drew is fine." He was confused; first names seemed so incongruous.

Dr. Peterson sensed some of this and seemed mildly amused as a half smile played about his lips. "Mr. Parelli, Drew, when I cautioned Ms. Beech to use discretion in her assessments I really didn't expect her to be so secretive."

Ms. Beech nodded and said, "We each carry out our tasks in our own way, Dr. Peterson."

"Yes, well, Ms. Beech has submitted a very positive report on your abilities as a teacher. She mentions particularly some of your innovative methods of motivating children."

Drew was struck dumb and could only look from one to the other as if this was some morbid joke he wasn't in on. Dr. Peterson continued, "As a result of her report, based on close observation, Ms. Beech has requested that you be assigned as lead teacher for your grade level. We've decided that with seven fourth-grade teachers there was a little too much disparity in what was being taught in the various classes."

Drew still looked dazed as he nodded.

"You will be curriculum coordinator for that grade in your building, and I expect you to act as mentor for the younger, less experienced staff," Ms. Beech interjected. "Since you will be playing catch-up in many ways, for the beginning of this school year, Dr. Peterson has agreed to make the yearly stipend retroactive to September."

"Stipend?" Drew croaked.

Dr. Peterson smiled, "Since you are so close, credit-wise, to your Masters degree we thought you should move to step eight on the Masters level. You should be able to take the final three credits in the spring semester. Next year the Board plans to institute a stipend for lead teachers comparable to department chairmen at the high schools."

The rest of the meeting was a jumble of questions and clarification that Drew barely remembered. It came back to him in bits and pieces as he tried to relate it all to Linda. But in the final analysis it only threw another stone into the already muddied decision pond.

— • • ● • • —

Linda had just tucked Kevin in and the baby had been asleep for an hour. The house was quiet. They sat at the kitchen table, coffee cups half empty and growing cold. Drew had the calculator out, and the yellow pads were covered with splashes of figures.

"As I see it, the jump in pay at school won't quite cover what I make working with Bill Knight. Maybe next year, if the Board comes through with a new schedule, we'll begin to see some progress."

"But Drew, you won't put anywhere near twenty hours a week on curriculum work either," Linda argued. "That means more time with me and the kids too." He smiled and nodded, pleased with that thought. She continued, "And obviously, they do know you exist in the school system. Ms. Beech, herself, recommended you for the job."

"True, but—" he hesitated, "suppose the stipend doesn't come through. Then what?"

"Oh Drew! You can't predict how everything is going to work out. Suppose the new contract for the apartments doesn't come through? At least this way you'll finish your Masters, and we'll be that much ahead."

"We'll have to lay out the money for the tuition and books. I'll probably get the tuition back if I can pull a 'B'." He stared off at the wall, lost in thought.

"You won't have to study and write papers between jobs either," she pointed out.

He nodded. It was getting ridiculous; they'd been over and over the same points since he'd come home with the news. It was Linda who finally stripped away the minutia to reveal the heart of the matter. "Drew, be honest with yourself. You know you will never be happy if you aren't teaching kids. Let's not make choices we may all regret."

And he had no answer for her.

—•••••—

Drew Parelli truly couldn't remember much about the next day at school. He felt detached, like an automaton, fulfilling his teaching assignments while his thoughts teetered back and forth, endlessly weighing the gravity of the decision.

The children were already on the edge of excitement with the approaching holiday. This last day before the Christmas break would be a half-day with much of the morning being given over to the inevitable Christmas Party. Class mothers would bring cupcakes and soda about ten-thirty and the festivities would begin. Linda always came and would bring the baby. Amy was two and the girls would fuss over her, delighted to be playing with a living doll.

Every year since he'd begun teaching, Drew and Linda had prepared small plastic bags filled with homemade cookies, hard candy and M&M's for each of the children in his class. Each bag held a small trinket — barrettes and hair ribbons for the girls, key rings with magnifying lenses or puzzles or whistles for the boys. Bags for the girls were tied with red plastic ribbon, those for the boys with green ribbon. Drew would don a red Santa hat with a long tail to distribute the bags of goodies. For Drew and Linda it had become a tradition, a ritual they looked forward to each year. This year it seemed even more poignant for them.

Sometimes it's uncanny how some small, seemingly insignificant incident can become the pivotal point on which something of consequence can turn. One such incident on this Christmas eve was about to unfold.

The children were already having their cake and soda, desks arranged in a circle in the classroom and happily chattering away. They were waiting for Drew to make the rounds with the little bags of goodies they'd heard about from the fifth graders. Drew was well-liked by his pupils. He had been tested, as every teacher is tested at the beginning of a school year, and had not been found wanting. He was demanding but fair, and he cared about them. And they knew it. So there was high jinx and banter as he made his way around the circle of desks. He passed out the colorful bags, teasing and being teased in turn at each desk. When they were all gone, he went to sit beside Linda amid the hub-bub and chatter as the children examined and compared their treasures.

Suddenly, out of nowhere, for he never saw her coming, Kristal Scruggs was standing alongside his chair. She clutched the plastic bag closely and stared at him for a moment.

Then she threw her arms around his neck and hugged him tightly for a few seconds. And then she was gone, back to her desk without uttering a word. It all happened so quickly that almost no one saw it, but Linda did and her eyes welled up with tears as she and Drew exchanged glances.

Mr. Parelli became the fourth-grade lead teacher that year and enrolled for his final three credits at the University. He still worked with Bill Knight on occasion, but there was never again any doubts about what his life's work would be.

The Outsider

I'm sure you've all met or known people who have just turned you off. No specific reason, just something about them you couldn't quite fathom that seemed to generate a negative reaction. Henry Emerick was just such a person. At first I felt a little guilty about avoiding him, but the feeling faded and I came to accept my avoidance without qualms of conscience. At first I thought it was just me until I began to observe his interactions with his other co-workers.

If I tried to be specific about what I found objectionable, I was unable to do so. That's what made the whole affair so ridiculous. Instead I found myself listing positive attributes, and that only led to confusion and frustration. Maybe it was because he seemed so bland, so nondescript, that everyone turned away from him.

Describing Henry Emerick was difficult since he seemed so utterly ordinary. There was nothing interesting about his appearance or his personality that set him apart, that gave him some modicum of distinction. On close observation, when I pushed myself to observe closely, he had a pleasant smile and a quiet way of speaking. Henry also had a soft, easy-going kind of disposition that seemed to project an eagerness to please. Maybe he was too eager and that made many of us uncomfortable, or worse yet, suspicious.

We all worked together at Ruhlman and Sims, Accountants. Our immediate group were all junior accountants, either having just become certified or having still to sit for the exam. None of us were more than a few years out of college, except Henry. He appeared to be a few years older than the rest of us. There were twenty-two of us, twelve men and ten women, all designated by the company as "Jays." Our desks and computer consoles were lined up in rows in a huge workroom ruefully dubbed "The Bullpen." As might be expected, we Jays did all the drudge work for the senior accountants.

Mr. Aspinwall was the office manager who parceled out the work assignments to the Jays. He was a persnickety little toad of a man with flat fish eyes, and a sour, unsmiling face. He sat in a small glassed-in cubicle in one corner of the bullpen. The cubicle was behind everyone so no one knew when, or who he was watching. As a result, the Jays were a tight-knit, clannish group, except for Henry Emerick. He was always on the outside, on the fringe of things, and no one ever seemed to reach out to him. He tried hard to be part of the small talk and camaraderie at the coffee urn before work and at break time, but somehow everyone seemed to shy away from him. At lunch time everyone left the building usually in pairs or in small groups. Henry never seemed to be included.

None of the women were more than civil to him, and one or two were downright rude. But, to his credit, he never responded in kind, and that put the onus on them. You couldn't help but feel sorry for the guy, but no one felt sorry enough to adopt the stray. For a while I thought he might be gay, but his feeble attempts to date some of the ladies of the bullpen seemed to void that theory.

Aspinwall was a mean, vindictive old bastard, and Henry seemed to garner a good deal of the old man's bile. And while we all did menial, boring work, Henry got the dregs. Old "Fish Eyes" came the closest to smiling when he was assigning garbage to Henry Emerick or, better still, finding fault with his work. Henry came the closest to acceptance by the group when Aspinwall was grinding him into the ground. But Henry was never aware of it, and by the time the incident was over everyone had his guard back up.

Then one Friday night something happened to change things. Henry and I got stuck late compiling some last minute data for one of the senior accountants who had a plane to catch. I finished about seven and was putting things away and closing down the computer when I was aware of someone standing just off to the side. It was Henry Emerick.

"Hi, Doug," he said, "It looks like we're both finished. How about going out for something to eat? I don't know about you but I'm hungry as hell."

While what he said was light and breezy, I sensed he wanted company. I found myself agreeing, and that was the way it began. I thought, what the hell, everyone else was gone, even Aspinwall, so no one would know. I was rationalizing almost before I had the words of agreement out of my mouth, and suddenly I felt ashamed.

We ended up in the Village at a little bar and grill I knew on Cedar Street. The place didn't have much in the way of ambiance but the food was good and the prices fairly reasonable for New York. At first the conversation was reserved, even a little stilted. Later, as we ate and downed a few beers we both seemed to relax in the flow of talk. The surprising part was that he was good company — informed, intelligent and having a wry sense of humor.

We finished the evening with a cab ride to my room and a half just off Sheridan Square, an outrageous extravagance on our salaries. We were at least sober enough not to walk the streets or ride the subway at that hour. The stream of conversation never stopped. It was as if the dam had been breached and nothing would do but to let the flow continue. I was suddenly aware that I was seeing Henry Emerick for the first time as a person. From time to time during the evening I marveled that this was the same person I had repeatedly avoided at work.

Some of the stories he told were hilariously funny. In retrospect, and without the beer buzz, they were poignant glimpses into a lonely life. Henry was an only child born to his parents late in their lives — and very much a surprise. His father was forty-two when he was born, his mother thirty-nine. He dryly suggested he should have been called "Oops!" or "Oh, no!" or even "Oh, damn!" From his comments and stories I had the feeling he spent his childhood and adolescence unsuccessfully trying to please his father and escape from his mother. He established himself as a misfit, an outsider early in life. His humorous stories of awkwardness and rejection only emphasized his skills as a survivor.

The capstone story of the evening was the account of his army experience. At the beginning of his sophomore year at college he enlisted in the army. By his own admission he did it to gain his father's approval. Nothing changed for him; he was as much of a misfit, a loner, an outsider, in the service as he'd been everywhere else, only this time maybe more so. For the first time, he was thrown together with those unfortunate people who could not sit out the war in college. For the first time he was in close daily contact with street people of every race.

As expected, Henry was mocked and ridiculed for enlisting, for having left college, for being where he didn't have to be. The blacks and Hispanics christened him 'Joe College' and laughingly, sometimes painfully, taught him the survival code of the streets. The white draftees were neither friendly nor hostile; they more or less ignored him.

In Nam he was a "grunt," but not a "bush grunt." As they debarked from the choppers inside the perimeter of a forward base they formed two ragged lines. There were twenty-seven infantry replacements and two medics standing hunched over in the rain waiting to be assigned units. The sergeant facing them was trying to read from and keep dry the roster list of new arrivals. He was shouting to make himself heard above the sound of the rain drumming on the tents and the sandbagged tin sheds of the compound. He was calling for a reader. Henry quoted him. It seemed important to the story.

"I need a friggin' reader, somebody who can handle somethin' besides a damned comic book." He paused and continued, "And if, by some miracle, he can type I promise him T-5 stripes in a month."

The sergeant waited expectantly looking from face to face along the line. A big, black soldier everybody called "Sweetbread" nudged Henry from behind and whispered, "Go ahead, man, save your ass. Make the college count for something."

So Henry Emerick became the clerk/typist for the HQ company. That meant he didn't have to go into the countryside on patrols. And for this he thanked the Lord on a daily basis. But perimeter defense was everyone's job. "Charlie" liked to come at night and did so fairly often. Base Bravo wasn't much safer than patrols, only bigger, with bunkers and dugouts for some degree of shelter.

The ironic part of it was that Henry Emerick didn't save his ass. A few months later, in one night attack, he got caught in the open in the eerie glow of a flare. The phone line to his bunker had been cut, probably by a mortar round, and he was stringing a new one. He hugged the ground listening to the whispers of metal as it passed inches above his body. And then he took a round. He got hit in the buttocks. The bullet passed through the fleshy part of both cheeks without damaging anything vital. Henry Emerick had literally gotten his ass shot off.

The evac chopper crew spread the word far and wide about the grunt who really got his ass shot off. The incident drew hilarious reactions from everyone. Medics and doctors and transients of all ranks made the ward where he lay on his belly almost a tourist stop. Henry Emerick had defied the universal admonition of safety and gotten his ass shot off. Even the Major and his aide had trouble concealing their mirth as they presented him with his Purple Heart.

The strange part about this narration, and those other stories he told during the evening, was that there was never any hint of bitterness. We laughed ourselves to tears at his description of the steady stream of visitors to the ward who wanted to shake hands with the guy who got his ass shot off and lived to tell about it.

——•••••—

Henry must have quietly left the apartment sometime on Saturday morning. I didn't come to until almost noon. I guess he slept off the beer on the couch. We did drink one helluva lot of beer while we talked. I thought a lot about Henry that day, I just couldn't get him out of my mind. I wondered again and again how anyone could accept all the rejections he had faced in his life without losing his equilibrium.

Was it possible that the Henrys of the world had been placed among us by the fates to allow a comparison, an ego reinforcement? Here was one of the nerds we avoided in high school and college, who didn't fit in at the parties or gatherings. We shunted them aside without a twinge, blithely oblivious of their feelings. I think most parents echoed my Dad's admonition: Tell me who your friends are, and I'll tell you who you are. Very often among the young this translates into don't run with the losers, lest you be considered one, too.

But if we are truly honest, and willing to admit it, there is a little of the loser in all of us. We each, I think, have a mental closet in which to hide our faux pas and blunders, things we are decidedly not proud of. We may look into the closet from time to time, but mostly we keep the door tightly closed.

Like most of my generation I grew up in a church-going environment but it was more duty than faith, I think. I've speculated about the existence of some supreme being who directs our lives, bestowing largesse and lumps on humankind in unequal measure. From my earliest years I was taught to feel compassion and empathy for those less fortunate, to count one's blessings, and I did. But deep within my being I harbored secret feelings of relief that it wasn't me. And I felt guilty until I realized I wasn't alone. It may explain the morbid fascination of those who crowd in to see the victims of some accident or disaster. Maybe the evening news has become a quasi-religious rite of counting one's blessings.

I chewed on it all that afternoon. I couldn't concentrate on the games on TV. Trying to read was even worse. Finally I left the apartment and walked across town to the river. The sun was warm, and I marveled at the indescribable crud floating by, but my mind never left Henry Emerick. Slowly I began to realize that I needed him almost as much as he may have needed me, maybe even more. The brief time we had shared had opened a whole new insight into relationships, even casual ones. It had been too easy for me to be a follower in how the group at work chose to treat someone who was different. It was a kind of discrimination, subtle but insidious, and we were all part of it, as much as we might deny it. I needed to shake myself away from that. I needed to reach out to him. He'd been an outsider much too long.

In an hour or so I returned to the apartment. I rooted around in the Manhattan telephone directory hoping that he lived in Manhattan. I found a number for him at an address on West 68th Street. There were listings for twelve Emericks: one H.E., but only one Henry. He sounded pleasantly surprised to hear from me. I told him I enjoyed the evening and his company and invited him to my parents for Sunday dinner. I suggested I could call my sister who was a junior at Drew to see if she could fix us up with a couple of dates with the ladies in her sorority. I could tell he was pleased; so was I.

All of that seems like such a long time ago. In reality it hasn't been that many years since we became friends. Now we share an office with our own accounting business. We share a round of golf now and then, when we can spare the time away from our growing families.

A Second Chance

Steve Fulcher waited outside the glassed-in cubicle that served as the office for the loading dock. He'd given his application to the first man he'd met on the dock and been told to wait outside the office. A tall, skinny guy had taken it in to the heavy man sitting at the desk. From the looks of things the man behind the desk wasn't too happy with what he was looking at. Steve had to admit he wasn't the all-American type as far as appearances were concerned. His beard and long hair tied back in a queue had been drawing stares since he had hit town this morning.

The door opened, and he overheard the last part of the conversation, "Might's well send the creep on in. Maybe I can convince him he don't wanna work here."

The skinny dude gestured with his thumb for Steve to enter the office, his hatchet face creased in a grin as he walked by.

"Come on in, Mr. Fulcher." The heavy man paused, reading the application, "I see Mr. Patterson sent you down to see me about a job. You know Mr. Patterson real well, do you?" His fat, florid face creased in a grimace that passed for a smile.

"No, as a matter of fact I only met him this morning. I was recommended to him by someone from up in Edgeton."

"Is that a fact? Now who would that happen to be?"

"I don't think you'd know him, Mr. Peters. It is Mr. Peters, isn't it?"

"Yeah, it's Mr. Peters all right. What makes you think you wanna work here? The job's a lot of liftin' you know. Besides that, you're out on the dock in all kinda weather — freeze your ass off in winter and roast it in summer. You sure that's what you want?" He paused, staring hard, "I don't play no favorites you know. I don't care a damn who recommended you. In this department I'm the boss, and I don't give a damn about nobody."

Steve Fulcher waited silently, offering no comment to what he'd heard.

"Well, if you're damn sure you can handle the work I'll give you a try — on probation, mind you. If you don't shape up, that's it. You un'erstand?"

Steve nodded. How come, he thought, I have to meet bastards like this everywhere I go? Like magic, the walking cadaver was suddenly standing alongside him, smiling a smile that held no humor.

"Just you come along with me, friend, and I'll show you the ropes."

"Slim here will show you what needs doin'. You take Mr. Fulcher and have him load those castings; you know the ones I mean, don'cha, Slim?"

"Yeah, Bull, those big mothers down the end of the dock. Right?"

Bull nodded, his little pig eyes watching Steve as he re-lit the cigar he'd been chewing on.

They walked down the length of the long loading dock toward a stack of large castings that were stacked two high. A sweaty little man in dungarees and a T-shirt was using a fork lift to pick up each stack of castings and load them onto a waiting trailer. Slim called over to him.

"Hey, Duane, you can quit loadin' those. Bull wants this dude to get in shape so's he can handle things around here." He pointed toward a heavy duty hand truck and said, "Any old time you're ready, Fulcher."

Slim and Duane watched as he got the hand truck and began to jockey the tongue of it under one of the stacks of castings. He guessed that the two castings in the stack probably weighed about five hundred pounds. He'd used a hand truck before, so he knew it was all a matter of balance. Where it got tricky and dangerous with a load this size, was turning corners and going up the little ramp into the trailer. He moved the first stack into the trailer and could feel the strain on the muscles in his back and shoulders. After the third stack the muscles in his legs and arms were trembling. So, this was it, he thought, this was the way they were going to get him to quit. He was slowing down now. The strain was beginning to tell on him. Slim was leaning against the fork lift watching it all. Finally he called out.

"Hey, you with the beard, that trailer is scheduled to pull outta here in an hour. You figure you're gonna be ready by then, or should I tell Bull you can't hack it?"

He and Duane were laughing it up and making smart comments each time Steve went by with another stack of castings. Sweat was running down his face and into his beard, and they thought that was hilarious.

"Well, what about it, Hippie. You gonna make the deadline?"

Steve never answered. He just kept moving back and forth from the stacks to the trailer. He had gotten his second wind, and while his muscles screamed in protest they did continue to function. He rolled the final stack into the trailer and turned to the two at the fork lift.

"My name's Fulcher, or Steve; I don't answer to nothin' else, so you might's well get used to it."

At that point Bull Peters came walking down the dock. He was a big man, powerfully built, but going to fat. His belly hung over his belt, and his head looked too little for the bulk of his body. He took in the situation at a glance, and there was a faint flush of approval as he peered into the loaded trailer.

"Well now, it looks like Mr. Fulcher knows how to use a hand truck. Ain't that nice! How'd you like to load another trailer with those castings?"

"I can do it if that's what you want, but it sure is a waste to let that fork lift sit idle while these two sit around and watch me."

"Now you just let me worry about them two. You just go ahead with your work. I got another job for them."

He motioned to the two at the fork lift, and they followed him as he walked away up the loading dock. The sweaty little man driving the fork lift gave him the finger as he drove by. Steve flashed him a big smile and bowed slightly in acknowledgment.

Steve lost count of the number of stacks he moved for the rest of the afternoon, he just knew it was a lot. His body grew numb, the way it used to when they hacked their way through miles and miles of jungle back in Nam. After a while it went beyond fatigue; you moved along on nerve. No one came to check on him, so he kept loading trailer after trailer until he was aware that Bull Peters was watching him. Steve didn't know when he had returned, or how long he'd been standing there.

"Well, you done right good. I gotta admit I didn't think you'd make it. But, like I said, you done good. You sure know how to follow orders. You can knock it off now. I'll be lookin' for you at seven sharp in the morning. Don't you be late now, hear?"

Steve nodded and began to walk toward the stairway at the end of the platform. He was acutely aware of how much abuse his body had taken in the last four hours. He walked down to where he'd parked his motorcycle and rode out of the plant area. Normally he'd have gone back to his room to clean up and change before he went to eat. Tonight he went straight to the cafe he'd passed on his way into town this morning. He was filthy and sweaty, but he was too tired and hungry to care. Steve returned to the room he'd rented, showered and went right to bed. He figured he'd get more of the same treatment tomorrow. In the not too distant past he'd have told Bull Peters to shove it. He might even have egged him or that skinny dude to try something physical. He smiled to himself as he stretched out on the lumpy mattress trying to get comfortable. Times sure have changed, he thought.

—●●●●●—

Day two on the job wasn't quite as bad as Steve thought it would be. He still pushed a hand truck around in the storage warehouse, but the loads were more generally suited to hand truck operations. He also met Edgar Jarrett. He'd been moving a large heavy carton along a narrow aisle, stacked high on each side with cartons and steel drums. As he made a turn into a side aisle, he almost rammed into someone coming in the opposite direction. He managed to slow down and pull back on the load to avoid hitting the man, but it had been a close one.

"Hey man, you need to be more careful. You coulda hurt me, you know." The black man was so huge that he literally blocked the aisle. He was so large, he made Bull Peters look ordinary.

"Hey, I'm sorry. I didn't know anyone was workin' in here but me. My name's Steve, Steve Fulcher. I'm new here."

The big man held out a hand that looked like a baseball glove. "I'm Edgar Jarrett. I guess you started yesterday. I heard Slim and Duane talkin' about you this mornin', called you 'Hippie'. They call me 'the big nigger' — but not to my face they don't." He grinned. "They a coupl'a piss ants. Spend most of their time suckin' up to old Bull Peters. Don't neither one'a them do much work around here. You just better keep your eye out for them. They'll screw you up in a heartbeat, just outta pure meanness. They figure old Bull will look out after them, and he does."

Steve nodded. "Thanks for the tip. I'll be sure to watch my back. It's something I'm sorta used to, I guess."

Edgar ambled off down the aisle calling back, "See you at lunch break."

Later, as the lunch whistle sounded, Steve went to wash up and get his lunch bag from the shelf next to the time clock. He walked out onto the loading dock and sat on some low crates. He started to open the bag of food he had picked up at breakfast, and he caught the odor. There was no mistaking it; someone had put a plastic bag of dog turds into his lunch bag. He glanced up to catch Slim and Duane trying to watch him without being obvious. Slim leaned over and whispered something to Bull Peters, and they all had a good laugh. Steve quietly dumped the lunch into the trash and walked over to the Coke machine.

Edgar came out of the time clock shack and came to sit alongside Steve. "Screwed up your lunch, did they?"

Steve nodded and Edgar continued, "That's an old joke they play on everybody that's new. If you get mad about it, they'll ride your ass right outta here."

"Nobody's gonna ride my ass outta here, no way. I need this job."

———•••••———

Two days later at lunch time it was Bull Peters who found the dog turds in his lunch box, and the eruption was about a 3.5 on the Richter Scale. Old Bull grabbed Slim by the shirt front and shook him like a rag doll, all the while roaring a classic string of profanity. Steve and Edgar watched it all from where they sat eating their own lunch. They could hear Slim protesting his innocence each time Bull paused for breath. Sweaty little Duane looked pasty-faced scared. Finally things quieted down and Bull retreated to his office, snorting and grumbling like a wounded walrus. Edgar took it all in and finally turned to Steve.

"Man, you sure enough turned the tables on old slimy Slim that time. That was neat, but it ain't gonna take them long to latch on to what happened. Now you really gotta watch your back. That Slim's a crafty sonofabitch." Steve nodded wearily.

The following day Steve moved castings again. Bull Peters came down to watch two or three times during the day but he never said anything. Steve worked alone all day and saw no one but Bull. The topper for the day was a slashed rear tire on his bike. He was wondering how he was going to get the bike to a garage when Edgar drove up in his pick-up. Between them they loaded the bike, and he drove Steve by a garage to leave the bike and then back to his rooming house. Neither of them had much to say. Really, what was there to say?

—•••●•—

The next few days were fairly quiet. Steve was still assigned much of the heaviest, dirtiest work. The big castings were again being loaded with the fork lift. Hand trucking them was definitely a punishment assignment. The rest of the warehouse and dock crew were a silent, sullen lot who went about their jobs without much talk or socializing. There was no horseplay or banter, no arguing about teams or players, and Steve thought it was odd. It was almost as if the were afraid to mingle with each other, much less Steve or Edgar. It was fairly obvious that Bull Peters wasn't happy about the easy relationship between him and Edgar. He never assigned them work in the same area, so they only got to talk at lunch, or as they were leaving at the end of shift.

Since the tire slashing, Steve had taken to parking his bike at a gas station about a half mile down the road from the plant gate. Edgar began picking him up at the station in the morning and driving him back at night after someone in a dirty pick-up made Steve dive for the ditch one afternoon after work. It was about that time, too, that another freight jockey named Walt Williams started the kind of verbal harassment Steve knew would ultimately end up in a fight.

It all came to a head one rainy morning a week or so later. Steve was drinking his coffee as he waited for Bull to make the morning work assignments. Walt Williams managed to jostle him in passing, spilling coffee on Steve and himself.

"Why don'cha watch where you're going, Hippie. You slopped that damned stuff all over my clean work clothes."

Steve didn't answer.

"Hey! I'm talkin' to you, Hippie. You gonna pay to have my pants cleaned. Right?"

"Wrong. Those pants haven't been clean in three weeks. The coffee might even help them smell a little better. I wasn't goin' nowhere. It was you who banged into me."

"If there's one thing I can't stand it's a smart-ass, big mouth hippie. What you need is a little manners."

"Look, man, I ain't looking for trouble. I'm sorry about the spill. Let's just forget it. OK?"

"Forget it in a pig's ass. I had enough'a you walkin' around here like you was better than everybody. Like I said, you need some manners."

With that, he stepped in close and hit Steve with a short left jab that snapped his head back. Steve moved away from the right hand follow through he knew was coming, and the fist missed his face by inches. Steve knew by the way Walt moved his feet, and the way he tucked his chin behind his shoulder, that this was not just another brawler. Walt followed him as he backed away toward a cleared space on the loading dock. He could taste blood in his mouth.

"Look, I don't want trouble. I need this job, and I don't wanna fight. You understand?"

"What'sa matter, no balls? Is that why you hide behind that beard — 'cause you got no balls?"

Walt was moving slowly toward him, and the other guys were lining up to watch the fun. Steve caught a glimpse of Edgar in the back of the crowd. Bull and Slim were just coming out of the office. He kept moving, trying to stay away from Walt Williams, aware of the shouts of the crowd egging Walt on. He wiped his mouth on the sleeve of his T-shirt. Maybe it was the sight of his blood on the sleeve; maybe it was just that. And maybe it was the culmination of all the other frustrations of the last few weeks. Whatever it was, he found himself suddenly ready to strike out. What the hell, he thought, go for it.

He suddenly stopped moving away and took a step toward Williams, dropping his guard a little. Walt grinned as he threw the left again. Only this time it went over Steve's shoulder. He stepped past the missed punch and slammed a right into Walt's belly. Too much beer, he thought as Walt grunted audibly. Walt threw his right but it bounced off Steve's forearm. Walt backed away, eyeing Steve carefully. Now it was Steve who was moving forward and Walt Williams who was backing away.

The rest of it happened quickly. Walter Williams had gotten more than he bargained for. He had an eye that was swelling closed, sore ribs and an aching head as evidence of his poor judgment. Luckily Steve had walked away from him after the second knock down, and Walt was just as happy that he did. The police car arrived just as it was over, and Bull Peters agreed to sign the complaint against Steve Fulcher.

—• • • • •—

Steve was ushered into the tiny brown interrogation room by the jailer. A tall man, neatly dressed, with thinning, sandy hair was standing on the far side of the scarred table. "Good morning, Mr. Fulcher. My name is Beasley. Mr. Jarrett asked me to stop by to see you. I'm an attorney."

"Did Mr. Jarrett have any idea as to how I'm supposed to pay you, Mr. Beasley?"

"He did say you weren't to worry about it, if that's any help. From the way he spoke, I'd say you really needn't be concerned. Now, if you'll agree to my acting on your behalf, we need to discuss the events of yesterday."

Steve nodded, trying not to let his surprise show. He wondered where Edgar would get the money to pay a lawyer. He also knew, from recent experience, he could have a court appointed lawyer, but he decided almost anything would be better than that. The court appointed lawyer he'd had up in Edgeton had done little more than stand alongside him in court and plead him guilty to an aggravated assault charge.

"I can't deny the fight, Mr. Beasley, there were too many people watching. But I didn't start it, and I tried hard to avoid it."

"So Mr. Jarrett said. Of course in the police report, Mr. Peters, and ah —" he paused to glance at his notebook, "Walter Williams both say you were the instigator."

Steve shrugged, shaking his head slowly. "What can I say. Edgar's the only one I know well enough to back my story. But if we are both outnumbered by Bull Peters and his crowd, I guess I don't stand a chance."

"Oh, I don't know, Mr. Fulcher. I suspect there might be some, ah —, extenuating circumstances. Suppose you tell me about the incident in Edgeton and how you ended up in the plant in Kelsoe. Elwood Peters told the arresting officer that you were in violation of probation. How did he know that?"

"I don't know. I was told by my probation officer not to mention it to anyone, and I didn't."

"Well, I haven't had a chance to get up to Edgeton to read the police report or the transcript of the proceedings in court. So, how did you come to be in Edgeton in the first place?"

"I just came off the interstate to get some breakfast. I'd been riding most of the night. It could have been anyplace. It just happened to be Edgeton."

"Where were you going, Mr. Fulcher?"

"No special place in particular, just heading west. I'd been working for a few months upstate. I just got the urge to move on, I guess."

"Are you a biker, Mr. Fulcher?"

"If you mean do I belong to a motorcycle gang, the answer is no. Never did, as a matter of fact. I don't have any tattoos, and I don't carry any concealed weapons, and I haven't had any drugs since I left Nam, and then it was only pot and nothing else. Anything else you'd like to know?"

Tom Beasley grinned, "Look, I'm supposed to be on your side. I'm trying to sort out what's real about you and what's rumor. Some of the guys from the plant have given you quite a pedigree. I need to know the facts if I'm going to be of any use to you. Shall we go on?"

"I'm sorry. I guess too many rotten, nasty things have been happening to me these past couple of months. What do you want to know?"

"First of all, what happened in Edgeton that led to a felony conviction?"

"Well, I came off the interstate to get something to eat. I stopped at this cafe on the edge of town, kind of a greasy spoon place. There were a whole lot of hard hats in the parking lot and in the diner too. I dunno if it was the bike, or my looks, or what, but this big dude starts talkin' at me from down the counter. I grunted a few answers, but mostly I tried to keep to myself. When it got pretty plain he was pushin' for trouble, I tried to get outta there. He stood in the doorway and wouldn't move. He was makin' statements about not wantin' hippie drug dealers around. I tried to move past him, and he started bad mouthin' me. He accused me of shovin' him. I guess I did push him some tryin' to get past him. Anyway, he swung on me, hit me a pretty good shot under the eye. The rest is in the complaint, I guess. I did a number on him, and when a couple of his buddies decided to deal themselves in I used all the cute little tricks I learned from the army."

"How much bodily harm did you inflict, aside from the cuts and bruises?"

"They tell me I broke one collarbone and one arm, not on the same guy. The big dude who started it all got his nose re-broke and needed some dental work. I got seventeen stitches in my head and a black eye. I wanted to plead not guilty, but I never had a chance, what with everybody testifyin' I started the brawl. Even the cashier and the owner of the diner swore I came in lookin' for trouble."

Steve sat silent for a few minutes, hands clasped before him on the table. He was looking intently at Tom Beasley.

"I don't want to go to prison, Mr. Beasley. I've been in jail overnight here and there, but I've never been in prison. The judge said three to five when I was sentenced, and probation was granted mostly because I was a veteran. He said he was givin' me a second chance." He paused a little and added, "What do you think my chances are of stayin' on probation?"

"Not good, Mr. Fulcher. Who was the judge in your case?"

Steve thought for a few seconds, "I think his name was Lewisholn, Judge Lewisholn. Mr. Oxfeld said he was a no-nonsense kind of guy."

"Did Bernie Oxfeld represent you?"

Steve nodded. He saw Tom Beasley turn away, but not before he could hide his look of disgust. Steve sat quietly as the lawyer made some entries in his notebook.

"Who is Edgar Jarrett, and why would he pay me to represent you?"

Steve shook his head looking puzzled, "I don't know who he is, but he seems like the only friendly person I've met. I really don't know why he's paying you either."

"Mr. Jarrett said he'd testify on your behalf. But I don't know how much credibility that will have in the hearing if everyone knows he's your friend. We'll just have to see how it goes." He stood up and reached over to shake hands with Steve. "I want you to know I'll give it my best shot, Mr. Fulcher. I'm not going to just go through the motions. If your story checks out, and I've been around here long enough to be able to find out, I'll do everything I can to keep you on probation."

Steve nodded, "Thanks, I appreciate your help. I guess I'll be hearing from you?"

"Be sure of it, as soon as I have something."

—•••●•• —

Tom Beasley came into the courtroom looking solemn and took a seat alongside Steve. Since Judge Lewisholn had granted probation, he would be the one to continue or rescind it as a result of the hearing.

"I don't like the looks of it, Steve. Peters and his two cronies are out there, all done up in their best, trying their damnedest to look respectable. Walter Williams is out there too, still showing some effects of your, ah– handiwork. Also I haven't been able to find Edgar Jarrett anywhere. He hasn't shown up at work since the day after the fight, and he hasn't been back to his room either."

Steve shook his head in exasperation. He was feeling nervous and depressed. He had the feeling it was all going to be a matter of formality and he'd be on his way to State prison by the end of the day. At that point, the door to the Judge's chambers opened and a bailiff escorted Duane Suggs across the court room and through another door alongside the jury box. Duane looked pale, and there was the ever-present sheen of sweat on his face.

"What's goin' on?" Steve was startled and showing his concern. "What was he doin' in there?"

"I imagine Judge Lewisholn was questioning him in private, but I don't know why."

"Can he do that?"

"There isn't any set format for these types of hearings, Steve. A judge has a great deal of latitude in how he chooses to proceed in a probation violation hearing. In fact, in this state, he could have just signed the papers rescinding your probation. But no one does that much anymore. Let's just try to stay calm and be patient."

Almost half an hour later Walter Williams emerged from the Judge's chambers, and the bailiff on duty escorted him to the jury waiting room. Mr. Beasley and Steve exchanged glances and resumed their wait.

Slim Brolly and Bull Peters came out of the chambers together some forty minutes later, and their expressions were grim. Slim had his head down and his shoulders hunched like someone who'd been beaten. Bull Peters suddenly looked like what he really was, a shuffling, sagging, fat old man in a too-tight suit. The bailiff pointed to seats in the empty spectator section of the courtroom, and they moved past Steve and his lawyer without looking at them. The bailiff disappeared back into the chambers and emerged in minutes to beckon Steve and Tom Beasley into the chambers.

Judge Lewisholn sat behind a large desk covered with an array of papers, files and law books. To his right sat Edgar Jarrett. Steve and his lawyer were directed to seats facing the desk, and the Judge began to speak.

"I know you both must be wondering what is happening, and I admit my methods have been somewhat irregular, but certainly not illegal. I needed to get some information in order to make a sensible decision in your case, Mr. Fulcher. I decided this was the best way to get it."

"I — we," he gestured toward Edgar Jarrett, "felt that granting a little immunity from perjury might help clear up the violation of probation charges. But I think I'll let Mr. Jarrett proceed from this point."

Edgar Jarrett's appearance was in shocking contrast to his appearance as a warehouse worker. He was clean shaven and immaculately dressed in an expensive, tailored business suit. The gold earring was gone, as was the corn-row hairstyle. Edgar looked like a polished professional, and when he began to speak it was obvious his role as a warehouse worker had been a disguise. He smiled at Steve and said, "Well, Steve, I guess I owe you and Mr. Beasley an apology. And if you'll bear with me I'll try to put all of the pieces of this puzzle together for you."

"Edgar Jarrett is my name, but, as you may have guessed by now, I'm not a warehouse worker." He grinned at them. "I'm an insurance investigator. I represent the Mid-States Insurance Consortium, and I work mostly on fraud cases. I was doing some undercover work. I got the job at the plant to try to find the reason for the uncommonly high rate of accidental injuries in the warehouse-loading dock area. The companies were paying a high rate of workmen's compensation claims, out of all proportion to the number of employees involved. I was hired through regular personnel channels, so no one suspected me. You, Steve, came on recommendation from Mr. Patterson and were suspect as a spy from day one. No one knew you were referred to Mr. Patterson by the Probation Department. It was unfortunate, but you took all the flack and harassment meant for me, and I really couldn't do anything about it."

Steve heaved a big sigh and began to relax a little. He started to interject a question, but Edgar held up his hand and continued, "Now, why the accidents and what was the cover up? Vernon 'Slim' Brolly was the prime mover behind a cozy little loan shark operation. Duane Suggs and Bull Peters were in on it and shared in the profits. The pressure for interest payments was jobs like moving castings with a hand truck and similar tasks which led to accidents and injuries. I suspect the management will find a goodly number of the plant workers in debt to these three. Walt Williams was an enforcer, especially for those people who weren't working directly under Bull Peters. I have been able to verify most of this to Judge Lewisholn's satisfaction."

"Yes, Mr. Jarrett, and your suggestion to allow each of them avoid a perjury charge regarding the fight was a good one. It has succeeded in exonerating Mr. Fulcher, and in no way jeopardizes the loan sharking charges.

"Mr. Fulcher, I am going to continue your probation, but only until the County Prosecutor can begin an investigation of the incident at the diner which led to your conviction. If there is any evidence to indicate you may have been provoked into defending yourself, I intend to reopen the case. I've been hearing some negative reports about that establishment. Now, is there anything you, or Mr. Beasley want to say?"

"No sir, except to thank you and Edgar — Mr. Jarrett."

"Edgar is just fine, Steve. It has been a pleasure to know and work with you. As I told the Judge, you're a hard working, patient man. Far more patient than I could have been under the circumstances."

Tom Beasley was smiling as he shook Steve's hand. "Well, I guess you really didn't need me after all. The retainer Mr. Jarrett paid is quite sufficient to cover my time and expenses."

Judge Lewisholn, searching through the stacks of papers on his desk, said, "Mr. Beasley, I would like to propose that you do a little 'pro bono' work for the good of the County. Would you be willing to work with Mr. Singleton from the Probation Department to find a more suitable job for Mr. Fulcher, at least while he is still on probation? The background report I have here somewhere indicates Mr. Fulcher has the makings of a communications degree, if he decides to finish it. Perhaps we can convince him that Edgeton, Kelsoe and the County in general can be a friendly place to live and work." He smiled, "Lord knows, we've already proven we can be hard nosed."

Tom said, "I think we can work that out, Judge. That is if Steve Fulcher is in agreement."

A relieved and smiling Steve answered, "For the record, Steve Fulcher is in agreement."

About the Author

John Muniz, a native of New Jersey, holds Bachelors and Masters degrees from Kean College in New Jersey. He spent twenty-eight years as a teacher/counselor/administrator in the public school systems of New Jersey. He retired to Virginia in 1980 and thus became a Virginian by choice. He and his wife, Doris, live in Forest.

Military service in China/Burma/India during World War II, as well as a wide variety of part-time and summer jobs while teaching, have provided a wealth of character and plot materials for his stories. He began writing seriously in 1983 and has been active in various creative writing groups in the area. Fiction, short stories in particular, has been his main focus of interest. He has been involved in feature writing and was, for a number of years, a contributor to a local magazine. His work has placed in a number of creative writing competitions beginning in 1985, and his stories have appeared in the Lynchburg College Literary Magazine, *The Prism.*

This is his second book of short stories, the first being published in 1995 under the title of *Whispers in the Wind.*